The
Cricketer
Book of
Cricket Eccentrics
and Eccentric
Behaviour

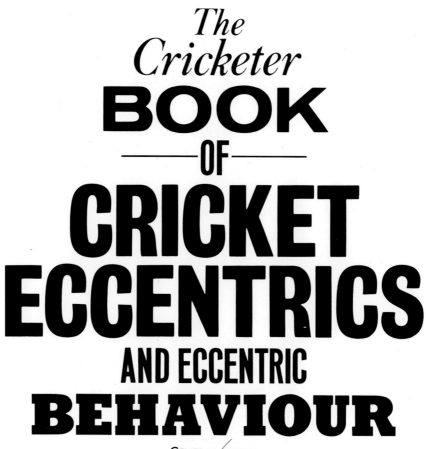

The Cricketer BOOK OF CRICKET ECCENTRICS AND ECCENTRIC BEHAVIOUR

GENERAL EDITOR
CHRISTOPHER MARTIN-JENKINS
INTRODUCED BY
ALAN GIBSON
ILLUSTRATIONS BY
DAVID HUGHES
COMPILED BY
CHRIS RHYS

CENTURY PUBLISHING
L O N D O N

ALSO AVAILABLE FROM CENTURY

THE CRICKETER BOOK OF CRICKET DISASTERS AND BIZARRE RECORDS
Christopher Martin-Jenkins

CRICKET – A WAY OF LIFE
Christopher Martin-Jenkins

First published in Great Britain by
Century Publishing Co Ltd,
Portland House, 12–13 Greek Street, London W1V 5LE

Martin-Jenkins, Christopher
The Cricketer book of cricket eccentrics and
eccentric behaviour
1. Cricket – Anecdotes, facetiae, satire etc
I. Title
796.35'8'0207 GV919

ISBN 0 7126 0716 1

Made by Lennard Books
Mackerye End
Harpenden, Herts AL5 5DR

Editor Michael Leitch
Designed by David Pocknell's Company Ltd
Production Reynolds Clark Associates Ltd
Printed and bound in Great Britain by
Butler & Tanner, Ltd, Frome, Somerset

CONTENTS

INTRODUCTION

Once I was asked to Monkton Combe School, which two of my sons attended (the younger was still in residence) to judge a speaking competition, or something of the kind. I can't remember the details, though I know that one of my colleagues in judgment was John Mason, now the distinguished Rugby correspondent of *The Daily Telegraph*. Possibly we had taken in an encouraging glass or two on the way. Such occasions tend to be boring, so I did my best to be lively as well as fair in my summing-up. I cannot pretend that I approached Gussie Fink-Nottle (on a similar occasion) and his description of how Bertie Wooster split his trousers, but the address seemed to go down acceptably with at least the junior classes. It was some days before I met my younger son again, and I inquired whether my performance had been satisfactory.

'H'm,' he said. 'More or less, I think. Someone did say: "Bit of an eccentric, the old man, what?"'

I took this, on the whole, as a compliment. I was reminded of the occasion, when I was asked to write an introduction to this book. It also occurred to me that I did not quite know what the word 'eccentric' meant, so I turned to my trusted friend, the *Complete Oxford*. Here are some of its definitions:

'Not concentric with another circle.' 'Not centrally placed; not passing through the centre.' 'Not referable to a fixed centre.' 'Regulated by no central control.' (Of persons): 'irregular', 'anomalous', 'capricious', 'odd', 'whimsical'.

So we have a wide field of choice. Probably more cricketers, at one time and another, have fulfilled one or other of these definitions than have not. Indeed, the majority of the world's population would consider cricket itself a form of eccentricity. All I can offer, therefore, by way of an introduction, is a handful of examples which have stayed in my mind.

Peter Hilton was an eccentric, at least when it came to cricket. He was a brilliant mathematician, and no doubt still is, but I lost touch with him when, after various senior professorships in this country, he became part of what we used to call the 'brain drain' to the United States. I was at Oxford with Peter, and one summer vacation we were members together of a touring side, the Oxford Crocodiles. I do not think that Peter had ever played cricket before, though he was familiar with it, and often to be seen in the Parks. It was the kind of touring side with a few good players, sufficient for respectability, and a number of others chosen primarily for their social qualities.

One day we were in trouble against a Devon village side, Haytor Vale. They had a formidable fast bowler, and a bumpy pitch, and none of our 'cracks' came off. Peter, last man, had to go in to face the last over. He knew the usual stuff about 'keep the bat in the blockhole, don't move it, and it can't hit the wicket'. But with a few swift calculations, he decided that to achieve this effect, the best place to ground the bat was 16.8 (or something) inches outside the crease. So he measured the distance, and took guard there, stretching out his back leg so that he could not be stumped. He also knew that the danger in this theory was that the batsman might, at the last moment, be tempted to lunge at the ball. To avoid this possibility, he directed his gaze firmly at first slip. The bowler was eventually persuaded to bowl. Five times did the ball smack against Peter's unyielding bat.

I wish the story had a happy ending. The last ball just nudged the shoulder of the bat, and he was caught at slip, in which direction his eyes were still devotedly fixed.

In the next match, he used a different theory. He had one ball, and hit it for six – a whacker, which won the match. In the one after that, as he was about to go in, a fellow-mathematician inquired: 'Is it the static or the dynamic today?'

If we think of cricketers of a higher class, the one to whom the word 'eccentric' has been most frequently applied must be **George Gunn,** of Nottinghamshire. I suppose nowadays it is necessary to remind people about George Gunn, so I mention that he played in 15 Tests, scoring 1,120 runs at an average of 40, and in all his first-class career, which lasted from 1902 to 1932, scored more than 35,000 runs at an average of 35. It has often been said that he would have played in many more Tests, and scored many more runs, had he taken the game more seriously, but one cannot be sure of this. Had he tried to play in a more orthodox manner, his wayward genius might have left him. He used, sometimes, to invite the slips to nominate which stroke he should play next, irrespective of what the ball might turn out to be. On one occasion, he batted with command and composure for an hour or so, then gave his wicket away. When his captain asked him what the hell he thought he was doing, George replied respectfully: 'Too hot, sir.' Cardus wrote one of his best essays about him: 'O Rare George Gunn!' Why does nobody write a life of him, when so many lesser cricketers are allowed such large, boring tomes? I suppose because genius requires genius to do it justice.

There was another interesting Nottinghamshire opener, a little later, **C.B. Harris,** one of the game's best conversationalists. Robertson-Glasgow wrote affectionately of him that 'he sometimes likes to act as his own commentator and critic. Having played and missed at a ball, he is heard to remark: "At Trent Bridge yesterday Harris was below form; his footwork was slow and his strokes not suited to the occasion." Or, in times of unusual disappointment; "Oh Harris, Harris, what has come over you?" ' But Robertson-Glasgow concludes, sadly, that 'I think he would like to be another George Gunn. But George Gunn occurs only in the singular . . . He has made the mistake of deserting art for artiness.' This is a mistake common to many who have vaguely sought eccentricity. It is something that happens *to* you, not something you can set out to achieve.

It was at Trent Bridge, also, that an eccentric incident occurred, though it involved two emphatically normal characters, **Colin McCool** and **Brian Langford.** McCool had made his reputation as a leg-spinner, years before, in Australia. Now, in his autumn, Somerset used him principally as a batsman. He would complain about not getting enough bowling. When the pitch was helping spin, it was Langford, with off-breaks, and MacMahon, slow left arm, who were given the ball. However, this day McCool was on at Trent Bridge, and a Nottinghamshire batsman took an enormous belt at him, the ball going high in the direction of extra-cover, where Langford was fielding. Such had been the power of the hit, the assumption was that it would be a sixer, and Langford, turning his back, trotted off to retrieve it. But the hit had more height than length, and before Langford had gone very far, he received a fearsome crack on the back of the head. It seemed that two deaths might occur: Langford from a broken skull, and McCool from apoplexy. But both recovered.

I could mention a few journalists: **'Beau' Vincent,** for instance, a former cricket correspondent of *The Times*, though his eccentricities did not appear in his prose, from which you would never have guessed his engaging habit of keeping his dentures in his overcoat breast pocket; or even perhaps my old friend **Eric Hill,** the master of the Taunton press box, the only freelance journalist who keeps his telephone number out of the directory ('I don't want these cowboy editors ringing me up in the middle of the night'); or **Ian Peebles,** who was almost as good a journalist as he was a cricketer. It was Peebles who was once prevented from playing in a Test match because of the intervention of a Scottish kelpie, and who also provided, on a tour of South Africa, the unique scoreline: 'absent bathing, O'.

And am I allowed to include fictional cricketers? If so, I must have **Raffles,** who burgled the houses of rich amateurs the night before he bowled them out (*pace* E.W. Hornung); and **Lord Peter Wimsey,** who was known as 'The Great Flim' after his hundred for Eton against Harrow, and was arrested for murder immediately after making another century, for the company of Pym against that of Brotherhood (*pace* Dorothy L. Sayers); and **Berry Pleydell** (*pace* Dornford Yates) who knocked out The Butcher of Riding Hood with a fierce return drive, and later in the same season won the match for Bilberry against Cleric, catching a spy in the meantime. Plenty of eccentricity there.

And plenty more, wherever you look in the nooks and crannies of this whimsical game. You have a bookful of examples before you.

THE NATURE OF ECCENTRICITY: A PROLOGUE

There may be exceptions, but, if so, they are only exceptions which prove the rule that in none of the world's great games is a man's character so well revealed by the way he plays than in cricket. Cautious souls tend to bat with extreme care, impetuous characters are unable to resist challenges or temptations, staunch men relish a crisis and eccentric ones positively delight in displaying their quirks and fancies on the field of play.

Historically minded readers will recall that the sensation of the 1899 season was the Hampshire batsman **Major R.M. Poore** who

The Major on guard.

averaged 116 for the county, hitting seven hundreds, one of them a little matter of 301 against Somerset. A brilliant all-round games player, the Major in due course became a

Major-General, his Test cricket being played not for England but for South Africa. He continued to play a good deal of relatively minor cricket in England in his latter years, however, and when asked by some enthusiastic undergraduates during a match in the Parks in the late 1920s how on earth batsmen should deal with the frighteningly fast and fierce Nottinghamshire fast bowler Harold Larwood, his reply was:

'Charge him, Sah. Fix yer bayonets and charge him!'

More heavy hats, worn in India by Lord Tennyson and W.J. Edrich, going out to bat against Sind in 1937.

On warm days the Major-General would play in a solar topee, and Ian Peebles recalled how on one occasion he was standing at mid-off during an MCC match in the West Country whilst the Middlesex leg-spinner, Jim Powell, was spinning his way through the local opposition with some ease. One batsman in particular was clearly unable to distinguish Powell's leg-break from his googly and the Major-General turned towards George Fenner, fielding close to him in the covers, cupped his hands and boomed:

'Depend upon it, Fenner, we shall have a catch directly.'

Seldom was military prophesy more quickly fulfilled because at the very next ball the batsman aimed a tremendous heave and the ball curled up high into the blue yonder in the general direction of mid-off. At this point the limitations of the solar topee became apparent because the noble General was unable to sight the ball overhead through the hat's broad brim. He began to exercise steadily more desperate revolutions on the spot until, with an exasperated groan, he called out again to Fenner: 'It's no good, Fenner, I've lost the beggar.'

To which Fenner, suppressing his laughter, replied: 'Hardly surprising, General. Extra-cover caught it ten seconds ago.'

Another military cricketer of formidable reputation and eccentric mien was **Colonel 'Buns' Cartwright**, late of the Coldstream Guards, who was President of Eton Ramblers for many years and who played the game himself until he was well over sixty. I once inadvertently during a speech at Lord's referred to him as 'Major Carwight Cartwright' and was subjected for the remainder of my peroration to irascible asides such as 'Silly young fellah' or 'What's the stupid ass talkin' about?'

He accompanied the Ramblers to Corfu for one of *The Cricketer* Festivals and we booked him into the most comfortable hotel available, telling the manager that he was a somewhat peppery gentleman, but had a heart of gold, and would probably change his room three times in the first two days, but would he please look after him. We picked him up at the airport and delivered him to the hotel reception, whereupon the manager came mincing up saying:

'I have reserved the best suite for you, Colonel Cartwright.'

To which he replied: 'And what have you got for bloody cheese?'

The girl behind the desk said: 'Please can I have your passport?'

To which he said: 'No, you can't. I'm British. I suppose you will ask for my birth certificate next.'

One day Peter Lowndes, the captain, went to pick him up from the hotel and couldn't find him. Eventually he discovered him on his balcony with practically nothing on except a hat with an Eton Ramblers band round it, doing a little Greek dance with two cleaning ladies who had come to do his room.

An invitation was sent to him to attend the final of *The Cricketer* Cup. The invitation read: 'The Directors of *The Cricketer* request the pleasure...' This received a curt reply on a postcard (he only wrote postcards) saying: 'I am unimpressed by your invitation. It should have read: 'From the President and Directors of *The Cricketer*', for I am President. Do I bring my own sandwiches?' (In explanation, it should be said that the idea of making him President had been mooted in a jocular way during lunch when he had been a Director of the magazine, then under different ownership.)

During tea-time at the final he was asked to make the draw for the following year's competition. Because he found difficulty with his arthritic fingers in extracting small pieces of paper, we arranged for him to have ping-pong balls numbered 1 to 32 and Belinda, the comely wife of the owner of *The Cricketer*, Ben Brocklehurst, held these in a jug so that he could take them out one by one as the teams were called. This prompted another postcard which simply said:

'Thank you for asking me to *The Cricketer* Cup final and please thank Belinda for holding my balls.'

As one might expect, cricket in Corfu has its own special eccentricities. How could it be otherwise when to Corfiot batsmen the call of 'Ne' from one partner to another means not 'No, get back,' but 'Yes'? Many a quick single is stolen by the home team as English opposition, accustomed subconsciously to relaxing when they hear 'No', assume that no run is to be attempted. Although they are generally attacking cricketers, the Greeks appreciate nothing so much as an old-fashioned forward defensive shot which is always greeted by cries of 'Bravo' from the crowd.

One of the great characters of Corfiot cricket was **Kontos**, captain of the Byron Cricket Club. Kontos liked to enjoy his cricket and always went in first and opened the bowling, keeping himself on until the conclusion of the innings. On one occasion he misfielded on the boundary, which prompted some ribald comments from members of the crowd who told him in Greek that if he didn't bowl so much perhaps he might be better in the field. With an angry glower he marked down the culprit, ran over and socked him on the jaw! This held up the game for five minutes until the police arrived blowing whistles, after which the game was resumed as if nothing had happened.

Playing against *The Cricketer* XI he was clean bowled first ball, whereupon he advanced in a menacing manner towards the umpire who obligingly, if belatedly, shouted: 'No ball.'

Not all captains have such power over the umpires, though the best of them tend to have original minds. It was unfairly said of Sussex captains that the players followed David Sheppard out of faith, Ted Dexter out of loyalty to the club and **Robin Marlar** out of sheer curiosity. Robin was a fine off-spinner who learned his cricket at Harrow where his schoolmate John Thicknesse returned to the pavilion one evening long after a team practice to pick up some kit and found Robin sitting on the rafters under the roof. It transpired that this was the Marlar method of protesting silently at the decision of the cricket master to drop one of his team-mates!

More recently I played in a match which Robin joined about an hour late – like me, he finds it difficult to be punctual. Just as the bowler came running in, Robin's car appeared behind the sightscreen in a puff of dust. Out he rushed, already changed into whites but with his shirt hanging out, followed all the way to the middle by a huge Newfoundland dog to which he vainly yelled: 'Sit!'

Generally, eccentrics in cricket are of two types, the deliberate idiosyncratic and those who are unconsciously so. Amongst the former are the Oxford Blue **'Loopy' Legard**, who gave up cricket to play golf, in which game he is the only reputable player to abandon the stationary address and to substitute instead a two-pace run at the ball, accompanied by a defiant snort; and **Commander 'Wally' Hammond, RN Retd** (no relation, I believe, of his immortal namesake) who played a great deal of club cricket in the Hampshire area and who could be seen before matches erecting a tent in the corner of the ground so that his wife and children might be deposited out of harm's way, complete with food and toys to keep them happy!

R.J.O. Meyer, Somerset's captain in 1947 and founder of Millfield, built from nothing into one of the most successful schools in the country, was perhaps not so much eccentric as original, but his bowling in sides captained by himself after his first-class playing days had finished was, to say the least, unusual. Playing against Marlborough College each year, he would open the bowling with outswingers, switch to inswingers, return later to mix leg-breaks with googlies and orthodox off-breaks, and then complete the trick with old-fashioned underarm lobs. I made my first school 50 against him bowling these and thought he was being kind to a youngster, until I was told that he bowled like this every year and often took a hatful of wickets.

But to me the most loveable eccentrics are those who don't *know* they are so! From club and village cricket in the Sixties I recall **a left-handed opener in Surrey** who modelled himself in complete detail on Bill Lawry. Like Lawry he was tall and thin, with a long nose; like him he would chew gum and garden the

Bill Lawry hooks, and we can assume that the ball went all the way.

pitch between balls; unlike him he would usually be bowled in the course of the first two overs, always by an 'unplayable' ball. More recently I came across a similar case of a batsman who clearly worshipped Chris Tavaré. Every mannerism and movement were reproduced to perfection, including the prowl round the wicket, head down, and the slight bend of the knees as he resumed his stance for each ball. It happened that in the match in which I played against him his side were battling to save the match. Whether he could also emulate Tavaré in the latter's more aggressive style I rather doubt.

Many would suggest that Tavaré's England colleague **Derek Randall** is a deliberate eccentric. I rather think he was made into one when he became famous. Those who played with him in his youth at Retford Cricket Club remember a shy, natural boy who marked his first appearance for the club with an astounding diving catch after a headlong sprint. I first realized he was something out of the ordinary when he ran out Barry Richards by yards after sprinting in from cover and hitting the stumps with an underarm throw, delivered as he slithered along the ground on his bottom, so that he ended up straddling the broken stumps with his legs whilst the great Richards looked on in total amazement at the end of what he had assumed would be a comfortable single.

Simian scratch by Derek Randall.

I first interviewed Derek Randall at Lord's after he had played his first big innings in international cricket in a limited-overs game against the West Indies. He was modest to the point of self-deprecation during the interview and left the commentary box by walking backwards, as if departing from Royalty. I ushered him outside where he immediately put his foot through a large hole in the floor of the stand. His boot stuck there and he moved out of my sight with one boot still on, the other in his right hand, muttering embarrassed apologies. Charlie Chaplin could not have done it better. A few months later in India he amazed the guests at a very serious and formal presentation ceremony one evening by turning a cartwheel as he walked up to accept his complimentary tie! The Randall cartwheel, like the Randall fielding, became famous.

A final introductory word about one of the many actors who play cricket, often for teams like the Lord's Taverners and Sparks. (Such cricket was not serious enough for the brilliantly successful lyricist, **Tim Rice**, who runs his own team, the Heartaches, and produces his own annual Almanack – already, incredibly, a collector's item.) Often these actors and comedians fool around for the sake of the crowd. But the real joke, the real eccentricity, is that some of them take the game in deadly earnest, as I discovered when once captaining an invitation team at Cranleigh. My wicket-keeper, so I thought, was that most stylish of all the great wicket-keepers, the inimitable J.T. Murray. As Murray began preparing pads and gauntlets for our session in the field, however, I was amazed to hear a bark of fury from a very well known actor. I cannot say who it was, but he remains a household name.

'It's always the same,' he said. 'I arrive for these games expecting to keep wicket and some bloody Test player comes along and thinks he has an automatic right.'

He was very definitely not joking and J.T.M. diplomatically conceded the right to the job with the result that the large crowd saw a clumsy performance instead of an elegant one. But nobody really minded. Had not the Champion himself, **W.G.**, been similarly inclined to lay down the law?

When tossing the coin with inexperienced captains he would simply call 'The Lady' and then stride off to pad up, whether it was Queen Victoria or Britannia who landed face up. There are a hundred such W.G. stories. The Doctor, indeed, is not just cricket's most famous player, but also its most famous eccentric. May there be many more!

Christopher Martin-Jenkins.

CALLED TO THE WICKET

The great mystery of cricket is the strength and staying-power of its appeal – quite as powerful as any career vocation, and as hard to break out of as a hypnotic trance.

Tom Richardson of Surrey was one of the first genuine fast bowlers. In 1897 he took 238 wickets – only one less than all the other Surrey bowlers put together. Richardson put his success down to his extraordinary stamina, largely acquired by walking to the Oval with his cricket bag on his shoulder, and home again after play – a distance of some 14 miles! Eccentric! He would not have said so.

It is just about possible for an ordinary mortal to comprehend Richardson walking *towards* the Oval, the whiff of a day's unknown excitements ahead of him, but the walk home must have been murder. Unless, of course, Richardson saw the journey in a different light, his true home being not the house where he slept but the county headquarters; in which case, the overnight stop would be merely a necessary break in training, his official address a kind of half-way house which he would happily leave next morning.

It is the sort of performance which would surely make an expert in sports medicine break into a cold sweat if it was allowed to happen today. On the other hand, all the world loves a winner, and Richardson's routine helped to give him that extra edge over his rivals that is the goal of most professional and near-professional athletes in modern times – though perhaps there are not all that many 'hungry' English cricketers.

In mileage, Tom Richardson's schedule pales beside that of **William Lambert,** the Surrey all-rounder who reached his peak around the time of the Battle of Waterloo. Although in those far-off summers Lambert's fixture-list would not have been as full as Richardson's, he nonetheless made a habit of walking to matches at Lord's from his home at Burstow, in Surrey, playing a day's cricket and walking home again. His two-way journey meant he had to cover a total of 52 miles over rough roads, with, of course, a match in between.

Lambert, furthermore, was no specialist performer but a talented all-rounder famed as much as for his roundarm leg-breaks as for his excellent fielding and 'severe' hitting (he was the first man to score a century in each innings). As such he was greatly in demand for single-wicket challenge matches, and on one occasion defeated Lord Frederick Beauclerk and the underarm bowler Howard virtually single-handed. With his playing partner, the famous amateur Squire Osbaldeston, ill and very much out of sorts, Lambert outwitted Lord Beauclerk by bowling persistently wide to him. Wides did not concede runs in those days, and his Lordship grew ever more impatient as he flailed vainly at balls going past him just out of reach. Finally he lost control of himself and was induced to give up his wicket, thereby earning 50 guineas for the Lambert-Osbaldeston partnership.

A modern Lambert might also live in Burstow and play for Surrey, but it is more than likely that he would drive to the Oval, or at least catch a train from Gatwick, and no-one would think the worse of him for doing so.

LORDS

William Lambert strides to and fro.

Public transport was certainly a necessity for **Gerald Pedder,** who in 1948 felt an irresistible call to take part in a match at Ditchling in Sussex. When the letter arrived, he was working in Nicaragua, roughly 5,000 miles away, but he quickly sorted out some gear and set off for England, and arrived just in time for the match. He was disappointed to be bowled for a duck, but later, while stationed in Fiji, the old enthusiasm was still there when an invitation arrived to play in a match at Heathfield, also in Sussex – although Sussex was now 6,000 miles away from Mr Pedder. Again, he made the fixture, and is probably club cricket's most eccentric traveller.

So strong is their calling to play cricket, the prospect of being effectively barred from the game is a challenge that some players find quite unacceptable. The action of the Australian fast bowler **Jack Marsh** (not a Test player) was surrounded by controversy, and matters came to a head one day when Marsh claimed, and was given, the wicket of Victor Trumper. The other umpire, however, was convinced that Marsh had thrown the ball, and announced that he would no-ball him the following day.

Marsh got wind of the threat and clearly saw the implications for his future in cricket. He went to see his doctor and explained his difficulty. The doctor obliged by putting Marsh's arm in a splint and sending him back to the match with a certificate stating that, while fit to bowl, it was impossible for him to throw the ball with his arm in such a condition.

Gout, rather than a possible bent-arm action, was what afflicted **David Harris,** the great Hambledon cricketer. The pains were at times so acute that Harris threatened to give up the game altogether. Happily, he was dissuaded on receiving the offer of a large armchair in which he could sit and rest between each ball he bowled. Nowadays it is hard enough to hide a helmet on the field to the umpires' satisfaction, let alone an armchair, but Harris's reputation in the game was considerable and no-one appears to have minded much about the obstruction. With his chair, Harris continued playing for several years.

Another tale of true grit concerns the early setbacks of **K.S. Ranjitsinhji.** When finally launched, he was one of the finest batsmen of his era, dominating Sussex record

Ranji comes good, and makes it to the pages of *Vanity Fair.*

books and playing with distinction for England. By contrast, his early cricket was marked with little success.

At Cambridge Ranjitsinhji failed to win a Blue until his fourth year, and it seemed he would never make the first-class grade. Unfortunately, this was his principal ambition in life. However, economic resources were at the disposal of the Jam Sahib of Nawanagar, as he also was, and he used them to pay for the professional services of the leading bowlers of the time – men such as Lockwood and Richardson – who bowled at him for hour after hour in the nets until at last he began to bat with greater promise.

A proper start in cricket is what every young lad needs. And if his parents have Yorkshire connections, they will know that they must start by making sure the embryonic star is born within the county boundary.

Leslie Taylor, father to be, was convinced of this, and also deeply anxious that his child would be a boy and that one day he would play for Yorkshire. The dream very nearly came to nothing.

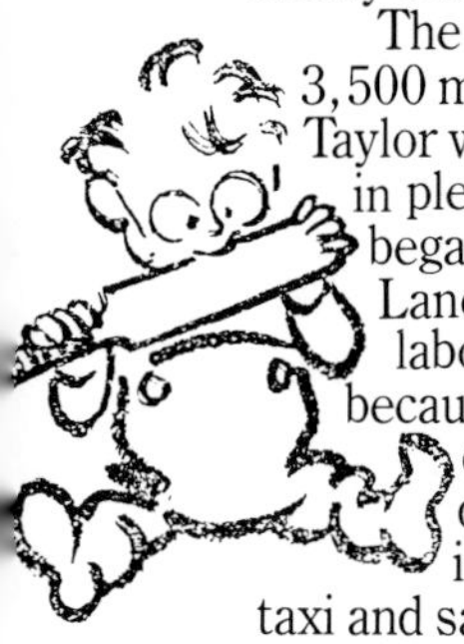

The Taylors were living in Bermuda, 3,500 miles from the sacred limits, but Mrs Taylor was persuaded to travel to Yorkshire in plenty of time. Her major problems began when, visiting her sister in Oldham, Lancashire, she found herself going into labour. This was all quite undeserved, because the baby was arriving three weeks early. To her great credit, Mrs Taylor did not pause to reflect on the injustices of life. Instead, she called a taxi and said to the driver:

'Get me to Yorkshire, quick!'

With her sister holding her hand, she made a thirty-mile dash to Leeds, and an hour later Duncan Taylor, as he was soon to be known, was born in Leeds Maternity Hospital. Only then, when the newspapers were alerted, did Mrs Taylor reveal:

'I'm getting quite used to this. I did the same thing fifteen months ago, but we had a daughter, Victoria.'

Mr Taylor was contacted with the news. From Bermuda he said:

'The two trips cost £1400, but it was worth it.'

The final word rests with the forthright Mrs Taylor:

'I don't like cricket. Never have. He can be a ballet dancer for all I care.'

They encourage a serious approach in Yorkshire – whatever recent Headingley-watchers may think. Back in 1938 **Arthur Wood,** the wicket-keeper, was selected as a last-minute replacement for the England team to play against Australia in the Oval Test. It was to be the famous match in which England scored 903 for 7 and Len Hutton made his memorable 364.

Wood rose to the occasion with the calm of a great general preparing for battle. He totally rejected all forms of public transport as unreliable, so hired a taxi to take him from Scarborough to the Oval, a distance of 258 miles. Eventually called on to bat, when the total was 770 for 6, Wood made a breezy 53 and, when congratulated by his captain, Walter Hammond, replied:

'You know me, skipper. Always a man for a crisis.'

MATCH BETWEEN England v Australia 1938
PLAYED AT Kennington Oval ON Aug 20
UMPIRES Messrs Chester & Walden SIDE WINNING TOSS England
SCORERS [illegible]
INNINGS England 1st

	BATSMEN	HOW OUT	BOWLER	Totals
1	Hutton	ct Hassett	O'Reilly	364
2	Edrich	L.B.W	O'Reilly	12
3	Leyland	run	out	187
4	W.R. Hammond	L.B.W	F-Smith	59
5	Paynter	L.B.W	O'Reilly	0
6	Compton	Bowled	Waite	1
7	Hardstaff	not	out	169
8	Wood	c & b	Barnes	53
9	Verity	not	out	8
10	K. Farnes			
11	Bowes			

did not bat. Innings declared closed 4.30 3rd day 7 wkts

LEG BYES / WIDES 1 / NO BALLS / TOTAL EXTRAS 50 / TOTAL 903

RUNS AT THE FALL OF EACH WICKET: 1 for 29, 2 for 411, 3 for 546, 4 for 547, 5 for 555, 6 for 770, 7 for 876, 8 for, 9 for, 10 for

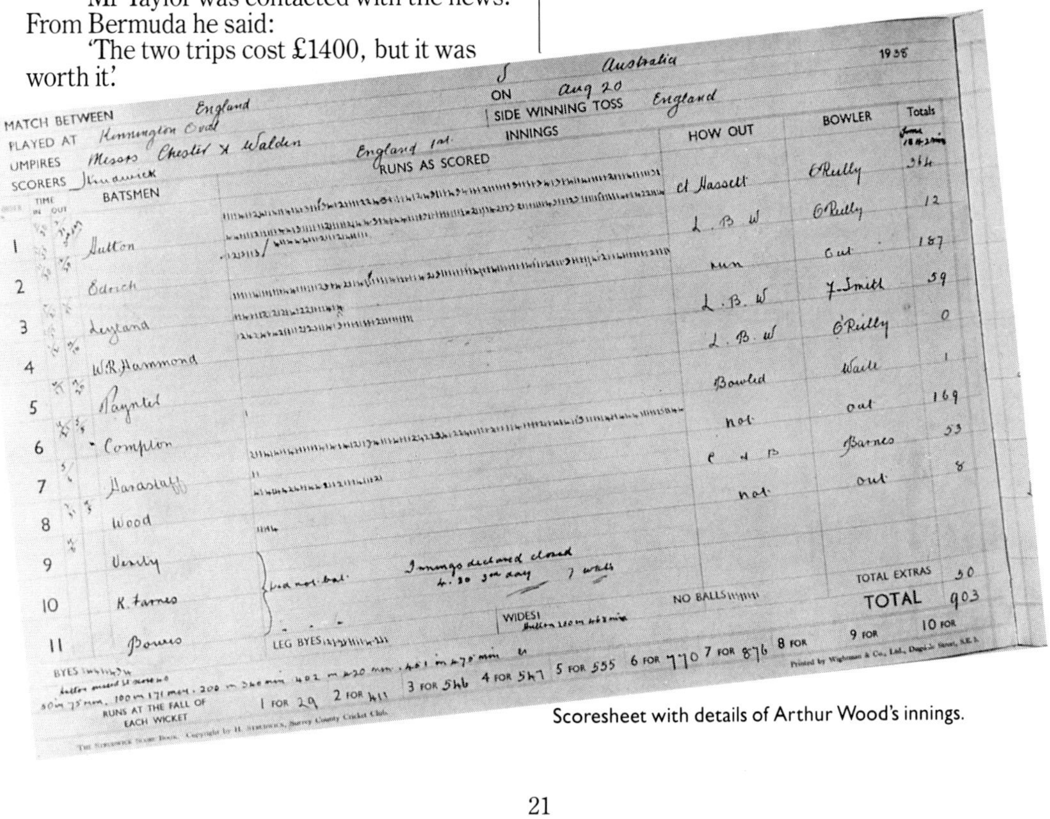

Scoresheet with details of Arthur Wood's innings.

Devotion to the cause knows no age limits. It was reported, for instance, on 31 May 1970 that **Wally Champion,** then aged 77, was still keeping wicket for Wallington. He first played cricket when Queen Victoria was on the throne.

On 8 August 1971 **George Beckwith,** aged 42, played his 750th consecutive match for Nutbrook Cricket Club. He had not missed a match for 23 years and even played on his wedding day.

The only player at first-class level to span both World Wars was the Kent stalwart **Bill Ashdown.** He made his début in 1914, and Kent were still selecting him in 1947.

R.H. Moss, of Radley and Oxford, won his Blue in 1889. He became a clerk in Holy Orders shortly afterwards, and played Minor Counties cricket with Bedfordshire until 1910, when he retired from the game. In 1925 he was called out at the age of 57 to play for Worcestershire against Gloucestershire. He had last played first-class cricket 36 years previously, and became the oldest to play in the County Championship.

In the Great Book of Cricket it is somewhere written that those who give shall be rewarded, if modestly. The turnout of the **Rejects XI** for the away match at Endon was precisely three, one of whom was the captain. He managed to win the toss and not surprisingly opted to bat, instructing the other two not to get out while he went off to round up some more players.

In due course nearly the whole team straggled in – not to find the game lost by 10 wickets but with their opening men still at the wicket and well in charge, for the psychological victory had been convincingly won. To gain precious time they had argued about the length of the pitch, changed bats and pads, complained about barking dogs and asked for the sight screens to be moved just about every time a run was scored.

Back at almost full strength, Rejects beat Endon comfortably. As their reward, the openers were excused wicket rolling at home matches for 'a period of two weeks only.'

Devotion beyond the vows of marriage is sometimes arguable, sometimes not. **Tony Seel** of Woldingham probably deserves an open verdict. His problem was that on Sundays in summer he naturally thought cricket, even when he was not selected.

One weekend his wife asked him to borrow a special kind of screwdriver. Seel left his house and ambled down to the pub, his mission soon forgotten. His club were one short for the afternoon match and he gladly filled the vacancy. It did not occur to him to go home. That is, not until he had been fielding for half an hour. Then, to his surprise, his car hurtled up to the boundary and stopped with a dreadful noise. Out stepped an angry Mrs Seel. She walked straight on to the field of play and deposited her husband's lunch over his head.

There have been worse endings. In 1981 the seventeen-year-old marriage of **Mike Rowley,** official scorer for Stourbridge CC for twenty-one years, eventually ended some years after he had left home to live in the cricket pavilion. His wife Mildred explained:

'Mike could tell you who scored what years ago, and what the weather was like at the time. But he hadn't a clue when my birthday was, unless I reminded him.'

Rowley admitted before the divorce hearing that he had put cricket before his family. By then he was living in the home team's changing-room, while waiting for a maisonette. 'I have been staying here, on and off, since the mid-Seventies,' he said.

He was not present at the divorce hearing itself: Stourbridge had a match.

STRANGERS IN PARADISE

Of all our European neighbours the French –
as a nation – may yet be the last to hold out
against cricket. However, just as there are
anglophiles scattered through that land, so
cricket has worked its magic in a few
unexpected pockets.

In south-west France, a French teacher
of English called **Monsieur Beneyt** caught
the cricket bug so acutely that he decided to
organize an English tour. He ordered a bat
from Selfridges, and arranged for it to be
copied by his pupils. He designed and stuffed
several pairs of pads. His coaching bible was
the 1950 edition of *Teach Yourself Cricket* by
F.N.S. Creek, and with it he tutored his squad
of players while waiting for replies from some
fifty schools which he had contacted in
southern England. Only a couple thought him
completely mad and so, on their arrival in
1979 in the Home of the Blessed Game, the
French team had a fixture list to be proud of.

One of the first people they met was Bob
Cottam, the former Hants, Northants and
England fast bowler, now the NCA Western
Area national coach. He took one look at the
DIY bats, pads and assorted gear of the novice
invaders, and told them to
throw the whole lot away.

But Monsieur Beneyt soldiered on with
his somewhat dented army of *batteurs,
lanceurs* and *gardien,* and gradually they got
the knack of things.

When he was transferred to a school
near Rheims, Monsieur Beneyt continued to
preach the good news and brought over teams
in 1982, 1983 and 1984. Their match against
Axminster Youth XI was reported by Scyld
Berry of *The Observer,* who noticed that 'one
of them gripped the bat the wrong way round,
most of them took off-stump guard, and one
opening batsman, Pierrick, ran out two of his
fellow *batteurs* in the first two overs, and a
third soon after.' The rest survived to compile
81 off their 20 overs and then: bravo! The
brothers Fabric 'put Axminster on the carpet.'

In Italy, **Alfonso Jarajaya,** an Italian of Sri
Lankan descent, acknowledges that the native
cricketers have some way to go before they
can expect great fame and riches. All the
same, more than 120 players are now involved
in building up the game. Temperament seems
to be one of the bigger obstacles. Says
Jarajaya:

'We are no good at building an innings,
we have no patience.' And: 'If a batsman
believes he's not out, he'll still be arguing
about it four years later.'

At present, public indifference to cricket
in Italy means that the pitches on which the
enthusiasts have to play are decidedly small.
This already threatens to produce a significant

regional variation, whereby runs are scored either in ones, fours or sixes.

Technical skills vary wildly. 'Our captain was injured fielding a wide', reports Jarajaya. 'He was standing in the gully.'

The image is familiar. Do we not all remember being eight-year-old demons, and on some holiday beach hurling down a screamer off a fifty-yard run-up which missed the stumps by the length of the pitch? The temptation to do so must be even greater among fiery Italians, with their macho culture. *Pazienza,* chaps! Lord's was not built in a day.

Some years ago, **a wealthy visitor from Tsarist Russia** was introduced to cricket at Merton College, Oxford. He seemed keen, and was offered a game with the Myrmidons, a casual eleven noted for their non-serious outlook. The Russian accepted with delight and asked what sort of equipment he needed. He was advised to come with 'the necessary implements'.

With joy in his heart he ordered a bat, pads, gloves, boots and a set of whites. By then his interest was really aroused, and he went on to buy a scorebook for 100 innings, a huge belt with a brass cricketer emblazoned upon it, and a large tent! We cannot help but

admire his sense of style, even if he was a corrupt and filthy capitalist.

The Revolution was a long way from bursting over **China** when **a gentleman from those parts** arrived in England. He became fascinated by cricket and decided to introduce it to his friends when he returned home – with suitable modifications. The need for these arose because the Chinaman was built on generous lines and, while happy that he could bat and bowl reasonably well, did not enjoy fielding, which he found too energetic.

Taking a somewhat cavalier advantage of his friends' innocence, he taught them a version of the game which had the ball attached at all times to a long string, the other end being tied to the bowler. How long was the piece of string? We do not know, but it was clearly short enough to make outfielders unnecessary.

Perhaps the string was *too* short, because in the inaugural match only two runs were scored. This had an adverse effect on the other Chinamen, who declared that cricket was futile and promptly retired from the game.

MISSIONARY FEVER

Since Victorian times, and even before, the world has been aswarm with soldiers, sailors, traders, diplomats, teachers and explorers who could not wait to put up stumps on every new beach and jungle clearing they came to. Even in the **South of France** a group of **determined expatriates** managed to set up a cricket club, near Cannes. Still more surprising was the eccentric location of their first ground – next to an ostrich farm.

The ground was rather small, and the boundaries short. The ostrich, of course, is a voracious snapper-up of stray cricket balls, and fielders soon learnt the importance of instantly following a six-hit into the farm. Armed with bats and stumps, they clambered the fence to chase the offending animal until it was surrounded and the ball could be prised from its reluctant beak.

When Singapore immigration officials stopped two Oxford University cricketers, **Simon Corlett** and **Bryan Hamblin,** they were under orders to protect the local population from 'undesirable Western trends and fads'. This was not a reference to cricket, fortunately, but to the players' unacceptably long hair. 'Get it cut or you will be deported in three days.'

It seemed a small price for two cricketing missionaries to pay, so Corlett and Hamblin went down to the barber.

The advent in 1921 of Glamorgan to the County Championship did not bring with it a dramatic conversion of the entire country. This was a slower process, but by the time the one-day game was established in England it is fair to say that the Welsh had a good grasp of current practices.

Still out there somewhere, preaching

Not quite abroad, but a novel cricket ground for all that: crew members of Royal Navy survey ships *Enterprise*, *Echo* and *Egeria* play cricket on the Goodwin Sands in stovepipe hats; the tide stopped play after two hours.

Split personality: William Pratt alias Boris Karloff alias
Frankenstein's monster alias a handy allrounder for
Hollywood CC.

and cajoling, is **Tom Cartwright**, the former Warwickshire, Somerset and England player. He tells a heart-warming story of our changing times:

'I got a group together in Aberystwyth. I said to them: "I've got a new competition for you," and they all looked up. "Yes", I said, "there are no league tables, no man-of-the-match awards, no batting prizes, no fielding prizes. Just a game of cricket played according to the laws."

'"Great!" they said. "We've never tried that before."'

Until its ground was bulldozed to make way for a million-dollar equestrian centre for the 1984 Olympic Games, one of the greatest of all cricketing outposts was the Hollywood Cricket Club. Founded largely through the efforts of **Sir C. Aubrey Smith**, the club's finest years were from the Thirties to the Fifties (missing out the war years), when the regular playing membership included such names as Boris Karloff, Basil Rathbone, Errol Flynn and David Niven. Not all the well-known actors were great cricketers but, as one member put it, 'like us all, they talked a fine game'.

Aubrey Smith had been a distinguished cricketer, and on one occasion – in the only Test match in which he played – captained England. That was in Port Elizabeth in 1888 against South Africa, and he took 7 for 61 in the match, helping England to a 2–0 win in the series. He was a medium-pace, right-arm bowler, with a run which began in a parabolic curve and earned him the nickname of 'Round the Corner' Smith.

His film career developed after he had spent many successful years on the stage. When he eventually settled in Hollywood, he specialized in playing 'typical' Englishmen of the crusty, patriotic kind. As the Duke of Wellington, informed of Napoleon's escape from Elba, he bellowed: 'Aaah, that blasted little Corsican is back!' In *Four Men and a Prayer* he was cashiered in strange circumstances from the Indian Army; in *Little Lord Fauntleroy* he was the old earl whose title was to be inherited by the small American boy; in *The Prisoner of Zenda* he was an impeccable, straight-backed counsellor. . . The roles were ideal for the man, whose behaviour on the cricket field was dominated by his regard for etiquette and spiced by his natural eccentricity.

In one cricket story told of him, Sir Aubrey was startled to find that he had just dropped a fairly easy catch while fielding at slip. This was late in his life (he was born in 1863) when his eyesight was failing. Sir Aubrey's reaction was to stop the game and call his butler on to the pitch.

Sir C. Aubrey Smith.

'Fetch me my glasses,' he commanded.

Play remained at a standstill while the butler withdrew and returned with the glasses on a silver salver. Sir Aubrey put them on and the umpire was given to understand that the game could continue. Only a few balls later, the batsman prodded forward, the ball took an edge and curved away to the slips where Sir Aubrey again juggled, but could not hold it.

There was a long and terrible silence before Sir Aubrey snatched up the ball and wheeled in the direction of the departed butler.

'Damn fool,' he shouted, 'you brought my *reading* glasses!'

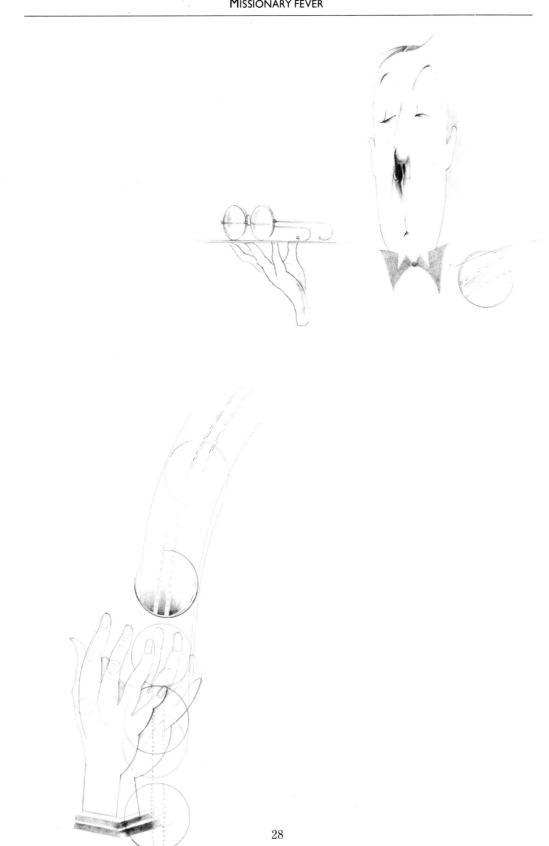

Missionary fever was not a major affliction for **H.E.H. Palairet**, son of the great Somerset batsman L.C.H., or Lionel, Palairet. H.E.H. was a sugar-cane farmer on the coast of Natal, South Africa, near the township of Stanger. Though now dead some thirty years, he is well remembered for his eccentric ways. A friend and neighbour, J.F. Reece, recalls:

'... He was a bachelor, rather pompous, and claimed to know the answers to many things. To his friends he was known as 'Puffles', which seemed to sum up his character rather well.

The distinguished father of 'Puffles'.

'Times without number he showed us, by means of pepper pots and salt cellars how he, with a little help from Admiral Jellicoe, won the Battle of Jutland. His farm would have been a disaster but for a good manager. His house was full of gadgets, most of which didn't work. From his desk he would pull one piece of string to open the door, another to switch on the lights, another to turn on the kettle. With furrowed brow and screwed-up face he would solve all our problems. He worked his way into quiz teams and could never answer anything. He dabbled in politics, setting up a party which achieved no votes. He organized inter-village bridge competitions, and spent hours afterwards on his post-mortems, telling us what we should, or should not, have done.

'What he knew about cricket was anyone's guess. I don't think he had ever handled a bat or ball, but may have read books on the subject. After all, he had a famous father.

'Came the day when Stanger CC was to play my school, Kearsney College. At the last moment the Stanger captain found himself a man short. In despair he phoned up Palairet. Yes, of course he would play. So he was put down to bat at number 11 and hidden in the field. My side was making fairly rapid progress and I had, I think, entered the seventies when the Stanger captain, in a moment of despair, called upon Palairet to bowl.

'This was the chance of a lifetime. Carefully he marked out his run, called upon the captain to make sundry field changes, to the nearest inch, held the ball before his eye in the approved fashion, lumbered up to the wicket and delivered the highest, widest, slowest, full-toss on the leg I have ever received. I slammed it with all my might, but got it rather too much on the splice. Nevertheless it was going head-high for a six when a somnolent fielder on the square-leg boundary suddenly discovered that he was about to be decapitated. He put up a defensive hand, the ball stuck, and I was out.

'As I walked back to the pavilion I passed Palairet, who was preparing for his next ball. He said to me: "I was bowling for that, Reece. I had spotted your weakness." I had no idea I had any weakness for hitting sixes over square-leg, but Palairet knew. For weeks he told his followers how he had inveigled me into getting myself out.

'Vivat memoria. He was a good chap and an always interesting friend.'

English missionaries go native:
David Bairstow catches a whopper off
the island of St Vincent, West Indies; in
India, Geoff Boycott hits the hookah, and
Ian Botham arms himself for some real,
and imaginary, game- shooting.

MEN OF THE WORLD

By our definition a man of the world is someone who recognizes that there is a world outside cricket – and actively pursues some extra-mural interest.

Several cricket people have found that horseracing gave them the connection they felt they needed with external reality. Umpire **Frank Chester** was such a man. One bright afternoon in 1924 he was standing at Taunton, wondering what had happened to his hot tip in the 2.30 race. George Hunt arrived at the wicket to bat for the home side, and immediately called for an impossible single. The stumps were thrown down and Chester had no option but to give him out. As he passed the umpire on his way back to the pavilion, Hunt said:

'I was only sent in to tell you your horse has won.'

Chester's most famous umpiring partner, **Frank Lee**, also had horsey connections via his brother Jack who was a great enthusiast of the turf. Lee was standing at Old Trafford in a Test against Australia, and on the first morning he was greeted by **Keith Miller**, also a keen betting man. Miller asked after brother Jack, to be told that he was in the ground that day.

'Does he still do the gee-gees?' asked Miller.

'Yes, he does.'

'Well, what's he got for the big race today?'

Frank Lee supplied the horse's name, and Miller said that he was backing another.

'My brother says his horse can't lose,' replied Lee.

Miller later changed his selection. In the afternoon Miller was bowling from Lee's end and had an appeal for leg-before turned down off the last ball. During the next over Miller learned the result of the big race – his original choice had won! When he returned to the crease at Lee's end he shook his fist vigorously at the umpire and said:

'You can tell your brother what to do with his certs in future.'

Next day a newspaper carried the headline: 'Miller loses temper over lbw decision – threatens umpire.'

Colin Ingleby-Mackenzie, the flamboyant captain of Hampshire who led his county to the Championship in 1961, was also keen on the horses. On one occasion he stopped a game at Lord's between MCC and Yorkshire. Moving to the boundary fence, he listened for the next three minutes to the BBC's live commentary of the St Leger. His horse was unplaced.

Bobby Peel, the Yorkshire bowler, was even less successful at keeping his work and his hobby apart. Peel's hobby was drinking, and after he had invested his benefit money in the lease of a pub, he was launched on the slippery slope. More than once he drank himself into a condition that was described in a report by *Wisden* as 'having to go away'. On one occasion Lord Hawke, his captain, banned Peel from the team for several days for 'running the wrong way, and bowling at the pavilion in the belief that it was a batsman'.

The last straw was added on what should have been a happy occasion. Peel had just made his highest score – 210 not out, against Warwickshire – and shared in an eighth-wicket stand of 262 with Hawke, who made 166. The following morning the slow left-arm bowler took the field after a night of celebration and, it is said, relieved himself on the pitch. It was too much for his captain, who banished him from the side for ever.

The temporary downfall of **Bernie Mason** was brought about by a mixture of drink, horses, and playing the piano. As wicket-keeper of the Jesters CC, he had set off on the club's annual tour of Sussex. The first match was rained off, and Mason took the opportunity to slip away at lunchtime to look up some old friends in Brighton.

At seven o'clock in the evening he was mingling happily in the Ship Inn with a bunch of strangers who had come from the local race course. There was a piano in the bar and Bernie, who loved to play, sat down to entertain his new friends.

By eleven o'clock, appreciative racegoers and others had plied him with enough liquid to send him into a drunken slumber. But now it was closing time, and no-one in the pub knew who he was or where he came from.

A quick tour of his pockets revealed that he was Bernard Mason, from Chilworth, near Guildford, some forty miles away. As the racing fans gazed sympathetically down at the sleeping pianist, up stepped a brave volunteer, one Peter Levett, who offered to drive him all the way home.

It was after one o'clock when the Levett car finally drew up outside the Mason house. Mrs Mason was roused, and Peter Levett gently explained that her husband was not hurt, he'd just had a few drinks. He in turn was surprised to be told that Mr Mason was not expected home, and that he had just started a week's cricket tour in the next county!

During a wartime cricket match at Lord's, the following conversation was overheard between a member and a reporter from *The Times:*

'See that batsman coming down the steps? Got thrown out of Eton, you know.'

'Really? What for?'

'For seeing his girlfriend off in broad daylight at Windsor Station.'

'Hmm. Bit hard, wasn't it?'

'Not when you consider he was only wearing his pyjamas at the time.'

The cricket career of **Aftab Gul** was dogged by political controversy. As a Pakistani student leader he enjoyed considerable power, so much so that in 1968 the student body threatened to disrupt a Test match against England if their man was not selected. The cricket authorities caved in gracefully and Gul played in the match.

Altogether Gul was capped six times for Pakistan, and his fine batting might have become the achievement for which he is most remembered. Alas, he continued to mix with political activists and after a spell abroad was refused re-entry into Pakistan. The government alleged that a SAM-7 missile had been found under his bed, and declared him *persona non grata.*

It was a poor fate for a cricketer – especially one whose name means 'Flower of the Sun.'

Until now in this chapter we have described men with various interests and occupations, one of which was cricket. In the case of **George Gunn**, that wholehearted Notts and England batsman, we have no record of any special interest that could match his concern for cricket, except his concern that he should be amply rewarded for playing cricket (see 'Financial Column').

Given that a famous letter from MCC offered him the chance of further earnings from the game, it is doubly mysterious that he should ignore it, but ignore it he apparently did. The letter inviting Gunn to tour South Africa in 1909–10 went into Gunn's pocket – and stayed there unopened until the party had sailed for Cape Town without him.

Absent-minded? Or was he eccentric?

CAUGHT IN A CLEFT STICK

On Christmas Eve 1938, **Reuters** produced a scorecard that, oddly enough, would surprise us less today. We would say: 'Oh, it's the computer.' But at the time, nearly fifty years ago, it caused a sensation. The news was from the Test match in Johannesburg between England and South Africa. The message stated:

'England
P.A. Gibb   not out   559
E. Paynter   not out   1009
                Extra   5'

In fact, Paynter made 117 and Gibb 93, so it is more than likely that a large dollop of Christmas spirit had got into the works.

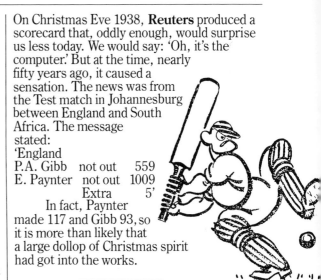

Many and choice are the eccentric misprints in our newspapers, caused by undetected errors in the production process. Other misprints result from mistakes occurring at an earlier stage in the chain – a bad telephone line, a copytaker with the stutters, an unchecked spelling. Then there is misinformation, the product of faulty eavesdropping, and deliberate muckspreading, or someone deciding to take a punt and to hell with the consequences.

Into the first category go these lines from a 1978 edition of the **Daily Telegraph:**

'Javed Miandad was the eighth to go. He was stretched well forward when a ball from Doshi raped him on the pad.'

Sir Neville Cardus, whimsical and original character, excellent and meticulous writer, spent much time trying to circumvent the machinations of Sod's Law, and of newspaper compositors and the Reader's Department. One of the devices he used was to send all items of punctuation with his copy – even if this meant cabling terms such as 'full stop' and 'question mark' all the way from Australia.

The pads of Javed Miandad were in no danger when he came on as a runner in this World Cup match against England; the batsmen are Imran Khan and Zaheer Abbas.

In the summer of 1938 Australia were the visitors to
England; Eddie Paynter is seen in action at Trent Bridge.

Two knights of cricket: Sir Neville and Sir Len at a luncheon to celebrate the publication of Cardus's book *Full Score*.

The practice was not admired by his cost-conscious editor, who dispatched a cable instructing Cardus to omit these unnecessary words. Cardus replied:

'I send punctuation, you fill in words.'

Sir Neville was at least once the victim of that misinformation we mentioned earlier, though which kind of misinformation was never established. Picking up a Buckinghamshire newspaper in 1971, Cardus read that he had died. He commented:

'I have no wish to challenge the authority of the Press. They must have some information.'

Another typographical error from the **Daily Telegraph** (on whom we are not picking, it has just turned out that way):

'In the collapse after the interval, the 26-year-old Prasanna shot out seven batsmen for 69 runs in 16 lovers, two of which were maidens.'

Here is an unfortunate extract from a newspaper report of a match between Essex and Middlesex:

'With the score at six, Knight had Gale lbw, and eight runs later Preston clipped one of Russell's balls about 37 yards.'

Had Preston been batting rather than bowling, the fault would have lain with the sub-editors. As it stands, we can be sure from the personnel that Middlesex were batting, so for 'balls' read 'bails' and confusion to the Comps' Room!

Eric Russell, the 'injured' party.

Finally, on the broader theme of cricket and newspapers, we reproduce this advertisement from a man who well understood the power of advertising:

'Refined gentleman wishes to meet widow with two tickets for Lord's Test, view to lasting relationship and matrimony. Please send photo of tickets.'

NO PRICE TOO GREAT

The great patrons of cricket have often been eccentric. Enormous riches are not the most essential prerequisite of cricketing power, though a few readies have always been useful. It is often a matter of deciding on which scale to operate, and then sticking to plan.

George Bayes would not be reckoned a rich man by Dallas standards, but in the Yorkshire fishing village of Flamborough in the 1930s there was little that was not his. He owned the fishing fleet, and was coxswain of the local lifeboat. He was, not surprisingly, *the* pillar of local society and much respected for his earlier athleticism, having played for Yorkshire at the time of Hirst and Rhodes.

George Bayes owned the cricket field in Flamborough, and the pavilion that stood in it. He owned the cricket club's equipment. He also owned the umpire. Lbw victims of George's leg-breaks were treated to apologetic looks and a friendly wink from George as they left the field.

'It's t'new law,' he would say, as if that made it any better.

Lionel Robinson's dream was to host a match at his own country house between England and Australia. First, though, he had to find a house. The funds were not lacking; Robinson was a successful stockbroker in London.

He was attracted by a manor house at Old Buckenham, some fifteen miles south-west of Norwich, which was owned by Duleepsinhji's father. He bought it and completely restyled it. He appointed Archie MacLaren, the former Lancashire and England captain, as his manager, and soon the place was alive with workmen laying out the new cricket ground; for the wicket, turf was imported from Australia.

At last the time was right to make an approach, and to Robinson's delight he was able to persuade the Australians to play the second match of their 1921 tour on *his* ground. They were matched against what was virtually a full England side.

The Australians batted first and were dismissed for 136. Between prolonged showers 'England' scored 256 for 9, including a superb innings by Jack Hobbs of 85 in just over 90 minutes. In later life Hobbs was reluctant to single out great moments in his career, but on one occasion, asked to name his finest innings, he said: 'Against the Australians on that little ground in Norfolk in 1921, with Gregory and McDonald bowling.'

Hobbs contemplates the camera.

THE AUSTRALIAN TOUR.

SECOND MATCH—v. MR. LIONEL ROBINSON'S TEAM.

By A. C. MACLAREN.

Our friends from Australia experienced the vagaries of the English climate during their game at Old Buckenham Hall, the seat of Mr. Lionel Robinson, who made all Norfolk welcome, judging from the vast attendance the only day upon which a full day's play was possible. Wet weather, with a cold biting wind thrown in, is always a terrible handicap to the Australians, and the irritating drizzles of the first day appeared to have chilled the team for their task when the game really commenced on the second day. The weather holding up after a short hailstorm failed to drive the players to the pavilion, Macartney, who was in with Collins, stipulated that he was not out if bowled off a snowball. The condition of the wicket is always a matter of vast interest to cricketers who are not there to see, to say nothing of the actual participants in the game, and reporters of the game who go to the players must be puzzled at the conflicting opinions given them. In this match I could not have said the wicket was ever easy, and yet it was incorrect to say it was difficult. It was, in my opinion, a very interesting wicket, calculated to put everyone on his mettle if he was to come out on top, bowler or batsman. No bowler made the ball buck as did McDonald, who bowled well enough to have gone through half the side in our first hour at the wickets, had not Hobbs, as the Australian skipper pointed out to me, been at his very best, and it was a nasty wrench to all present to see him falter as he dashed past the crease after he had treated the spectators to as delightful an exhibition of class batting as the Norfolk people will ever see. The same muscle which cracked in Australia had gone again, and it is not easy to put these troubles right in a few days, but we must hope for the best for Jack Hobbs' and England's sake.

To hark back to the early stages of the game, the Australian cracks felt their way cautiously on the firm if somewhat dead wicket, and after getting the pace of same, adopted a bolder policy, which was the undoing of the three first batsmen to the bowling of J. H. W. T. Douglas and C. H. Gibson, both of whom kept a capital length, the former swinging away considerably at times, whilst Gibson occasionally floated the ball over the blind spot in disconcerting fashion. Bardsley attempted to loft a middle and off stump ball over short mid-on, which he failed to get in the middle of the bat, and J. C. White, turning quickly, and sprinting all out, overtook the skyer to collect it after the ball always appeared to be beating him, and bringing off a clinking good catch, which fully deserved the applause of the whole ground which greeted it, Douglas being the bowler. Then Collins, who had been at the wickets long enough to show us what a nice player he is, tried to bring off a short-arm pull to one of Gibson's, which jumped enough to cause the batsman to pull it off the top half of the bat into D. J. Knight's hands at mid-on. Charlie Macartney, in the meanwhile, when playing well within himself, set himself to hook Douglas, but changed his mind, to be caught at the wicket off a cross bat. Armstrong and Taylor made a big effort to put things right, the latter playing them all in the middle of the bat, and using fine discretion in sorting them out, whilst the skipper, as one might expect, improved as he warmed up to finally play all his best strokes in a very meritorious 51 not out, finding no one to stay with him after Taylor unfortunately ran himself out in calling his captain for a lightning burst, which Armstrong rightly refused, after glancing the ball straight to Hendren at fine leg.

Douglas and Gibson bowled for an hour and twenty minutes before the latter made way for V. W. C. Jupp, whose first over to Armstrong realised 16 runs, owing to the shortness of his length, the intense cold handicapping the bowler, for it took at least three overs to warm up. After lunch, White bowled for Jupp, but the wicket was not quite fast enough for the Somerset man, who, nevertheless, bowled well, and Gibson

at once came back to get two wickets immediately, A. P. F. Chapman bringing off a nice catch from a genuine cut, and Carter falling in trying to place a pull shot. Douglas, at the other end, who bowled unchanged throughout, succeeded in getting Gregory lbw, as also Mailey and McDonald, both of whom were hitting square. Douglas, who bowled slower than he did last season, bowled capitally throughout, his swinging ball being responsible for his wickets in almost every instance. He gave nothing away in the shape of bad length or leg balls, and I am satisfied that he is every bit as great a bowler to-day as ever, and his determined effort brought out the very best from all the fieldsmen. Gibson could not have bowled better, and it was a feather in any young bowler's cap to have but 33 runs scored off him for three wickets in his 16 overs, the majority of which were delivered against their crack batsmen. Douglas, unchanged, took six for 64, and if these good figures can repeat themselves, we should hold our own. In the Australian second innings, on the slightly faster wicket, Gibson bowled 9 overs 8 maidens 1 run 1 wicket against Bardsley and Collins, with Macartney to follow. If any other bowler in England can beat this, will the selectors please produce one? Once again, may I impress upon those who are going to find the team to beat Australia, to tear up the book of form, and throw out those whose only crime is increasing age for our youngsters, who keep the game alive from start to finish? In this game it was a treat to see Hobbs, Hendren, Chapman, Knight, White, Jupp, and others, to say nothing of G. E. C. Wood behind the wickets, do really brilliant things.

In regard to our batting. Knight found a snorter, which whipped back for a bent knee in front to stop. Hobbs was at his very best. Jupp started as if short of practice, but went on to bring off many good shots on the on side mostly, and he certainly would have done our boys good in Australia. Hendren made some good strokes, if not on his top form. Chapman most unluckily cut under his first ball, but he will get many runs later. Douglas was dogged, and played that determined game which is invaluable. McDonald looked always a high-class bowler, who will get everything out of a wicket possible. Gregory not quite himself, with his shoulder muscles refusing to work in the cold. Hobbs killed Mailey's breaks on a wicket unsuited to the bowler. Hendry, a capital slip, bowled for a long spell, and might have had more luck.

I think just as much as ever of Australia. They are all batters, and the ability is there, but they didn't expect to get any skating this summer.

AUSTRALIANS.

	1st Innings.		2nd innings.	
W. Bardsley, c White, b Douglas	10	not out		8
H. L. Collins, c Knight, b Gibson	23	c Fender, b Gibson		15
C. G. Macartney, c Wood, b Douglas	11	not out		1
J. M. Taylor, run out	20			
W. W. Armstrong, not out	51			
J. M. Gregory, lbw, b Douglas	2			
J. C. Ryder, c Knight, b Douglas	0			
E. L. Hendry, c Chapman, b Gibson	5			
H. Carter, c Jupp, b Gibson	2			
E. A. McDonald, lbw, b Douglas	0			
A. A. Mailey, lbw, b Douglas	4			
Extras	8	Extras		1
Total	136	Total (1 wkt)		25

MR. L. ROBINSON'S XI.—First Innings.

Hobbs, retired hurt	85
D. J. Knight, lbw, b McDonald	1
V. W. C. Jupp, retired hurt	59
Hendren, c Hendry, b McDonald	20
A. P. F. Chapman, c Hendry, b Macdonald	0
J. W. H. T. Douglas, not out	41
P. G. H. Fender, c Hendry, b McDonald	10
G. E. C. Wood, c Gregory, b Hendry	2
C. H. Gibson, c Mailey, b Gregory	1
J. C. White, b Gregory	0
A. C. McLaren, not out	25
Extras	12
Total (7 wickets)	256*

* Innings declared closed.

How *The Cricketer* saw the match at Old Buckenham Hall.

ENGLAND v. AUSTRALIA.

Gregory and McDonald terrorized English batsmen
throughout the summer of 1921.

The house was later sold, became a school, then fell into disuse when the school moved to Suffolk. Today the pitch has problems surviving even as a village ground. Robinson, though, died a happy man.

___

More recently a Lancashire cricket enthusiast named **Tim Hudson,** who found fame as a disc-jockey in the United States, returned home to spend some of his fortune on a private ground in Cheshire which he has called Birtles Bowl. Long-haired, and with the look of a pop-singer, he has delighted in being photographed in the company of men such as Geoff Boycott and Ian Botham, for whom he organized a benefit match at the Bowl with a £10,000 prize to the winner. During the game 'Lord' Tim dispensed champagne and, according to Peter Roebuck, it was 'a pleasantly idiotic day with bangles and beads a-plenty'.

Also in recent times, members of a Kent club had reason to fear for their future when ownership of their ground passed into the hands of an Arab oil sheikh. For the last hundred years or so they had been paying only a nominal rent. After much deliberation and careful drafting, a letter was sent to the new squire inviting him to become a vice-president of the club; the matter of rent was played down, and instead it was cautiously suggested that a donation to club funds would be much appreciated.

When the reply came, it contained two impressive features: a gracious and enthusiastic acceptance of the office of vice-president – and a cheque for £14,000 which, it was hoped, would be acceptable!

___

The great days of country-house cricket reached a final and thunderous climax at the grounds of **Sir Julien Cahn.** His Eleven played more than 600 matches between 1923 and 1941, and in the Thirties they went on tours to Jamaica, North and South America, the Far East and New Zealand. They sported Sir Julien's own colours of black, pink and light blue, and wore dark blue caps with a fox's head as the badge.

Sir Julien was born into a wealthy Nottingham family which had prospered in the furniture trade. He indulged his passion for cricket by laying out two private cricket grounds. The first was at West Bridgford, near Trent Bridge, on a nine-acre site complete with a roomy pavilion which was almost a country house in its own right. In 1929 he moved to still more sumptuous surroundings at Stanford Hall in Leicestershire.

To help him, Sir Julien could call on a large domestic staff, but he also needed regular cricketing help as well. He solved this problem by recruiting a nucleus of players of first-class ability and either paying them a salary to work for him or setting them up in a local business which left them sufficient time to turn out for the Eleven when needed. The team was then topped up with specially invited guest players, who at one time or another included Ian Peebles, 'Tich' Richmond, Jack Walsh, Andy Sandham, R.W.V. Robins and G.F.H. Heane.

Sir Julien was a little strange at times, a little vain, a little rude, but in general his guests were pleased to accept their invitations to play and stay at Stanford Hall, and local charities also benefited handsomely from the generosity of the host and team captain.

Thereby lay the only lasting snag. Sir Julien was like the small boy in the park who owns the ball. Without him in the team there could be no game. Sir Julien Cahn's XI contained so many players of county and even Test standard that his own batting ability was regularly shown up as being a little weak. His slow bowling was enjoyed more by the opposition than by his own side. He also suffered from unusually fragile bones, but here at least he was able to use his financial resources to good effect.

Guests at Stanford Hall: R.W.V. Robins and, right, Andy Sandham

Sir Julien commissioned a pair of inflatable batting pads. These bulbous articles served not only to protect their owner's brittle legs but also as run-gatherers, for Sir Julien developed a subtle technique of 'shinning' any ball that pitched off-line, and this brought the Eleven a useful bonus in leg-byes.

The pads were uncomfortable to walk in for any length of time, and Sir Julien often resorted, with no apparent loss of dignity, to a bath chair to ferry him from pavilion to wicket and back. He later commissioned a second, less bulky pair which fitted under his trousers and which he wore for fielding. Mid-off was his favourite position, and such was the resilience of these fielding pads that a full-blooded off-drive could be returned to the wicket-keeper within moments of leaving the bat.

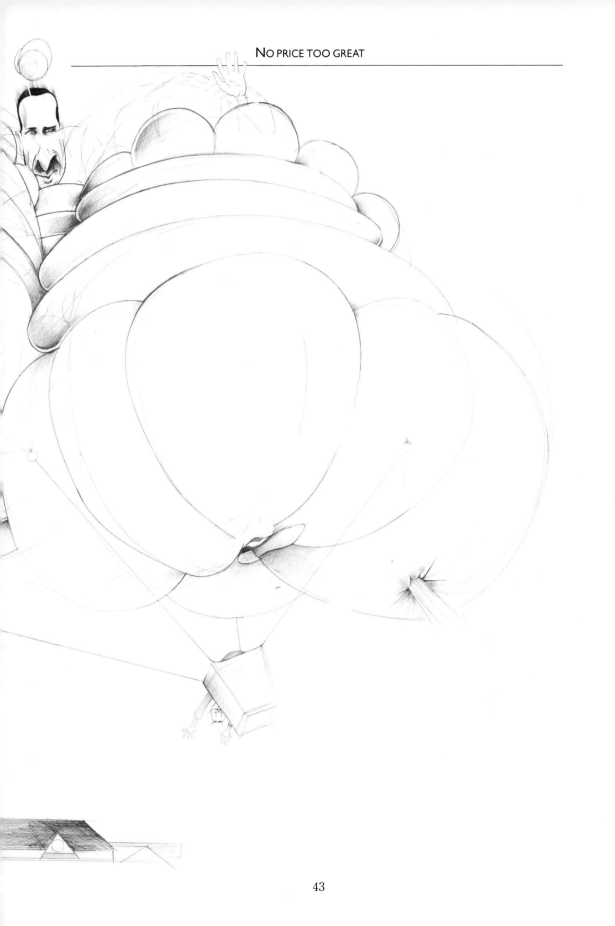

There is almost nothing more touching in cricket than the love of a good man for his *Wisdens*. **Philip Jones,** a Nottingham company director, was so keen on his annuals that in 1979 he paid £4200 at auction to acquire complete set from 1864 to 1969 – a total of 102 Almanacks. He already possessed a hundred of them, but had to buy the entire set in order to obtain the missing two editions.

Major R.O. Edwards would have understood. His obituary in *The Cricketer* of 22 May 1926 described how he had been badly gassed in the Great War. Later, in an expedition to Southern Russia, he lost all his baggage except the set of *Wisdens* which had accompanied him on all his travels.

What the late **Ron Yeomans** – a keen member of the Cricket Society movement – may have lacked in financial depth he more than made up for in enthusiasm and ingenuity. The lawn beside his house in Leeds was made from 23 cricket grounds. 'I used to take away two-foot squares of turf in a little bag,' he said.

Then he moved to a new house, and set about furnishing it in a fashion which hardly concealed his love for the great game. In the front gate was set a wicket from the 1955 Headingley Test against South Africa. Rooms were decorated with wallpaper from Sir Leonard Hutton's leftovers. He had a stained glass window which showed a Victorian cricket scene. His cat was called Wisden, there were drinking glasses with cricketers on the sideboard, and he – and invited guests, no doubt – could blow their noses on W.G. Grace handkerchiefs.

TALES FROM THE CRYPT

A country clergyman was addressing the mourners at the funeral of the local team's fast bowler. He came to the climax of his address with these words:

'And so we should mingle our sorrow with rejoicing. Let us think of William bowling away on a perfect wicket in lovely sunshine for all eternity.'

'By gum,' remarked one of his old team-mates audibly, 'that'll kill old Bill.'

Harry Bagshaw of Derbyshire, a first-class umpire, was buried in 1927 according to his instructions, dressed in his umpire's coat and holding a cricket ball in one hand. Rumour has it that his other hand was raised above his head!

Alfred Shaw, the old Notts bowler, expressed a dying wish that he be buried 'a cricket pitch away' from his old team-mate **Arthur Shrewsbury**. The request was respected, but some weeks later a local pedant pointed out that the graves were not 22, but 27, yards apart. The error was reported to the county secretary.

'That's all right,' said the official. 'Alfred always took a five-yard run.'

And now, the final score:
Quad-I-Azam Trophy final
Karachi 1958–59

1st inns	2nd inns
Abdul Aziz retired hurt 0	did not bat, dead 0

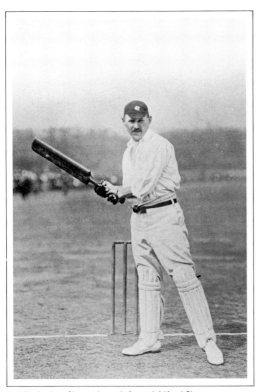

In life: Arthur Shrewsbury, left, and Alfred Shaw.
Overleaf: still only a cricket pitch apart ...

Bats out of Hell

ARTHUR SHREWSBURY

SPECIALISTS IN THEIR ART

One-day cricket has greatly increased the demand for all-rounders who can perform well at first-class level in at least two departments, and preferably three since the run-saving feats of a good fielder can win matches.

In more relaxed times it was not necessary for county players to be so indecently talented, while at village level it was enough to enjoy the game and take part – the results would take care of themselves. **Sir James Barrie**, author of *Peter Pan*, was one whose art stopped well short of cricketing prowess, and yet he loved the game enough to form a team which he christened the Allahackbarries. His own speciality was slow bowling – so slow, in fact, that if he bowled a ball which by his own standards he considered loose, he had time to run up the pitch and retrieve it before it reached the batsman.

Beaumont Cranfield, the Somerset left-hander who played at the turn of the century, had a special delivery which may have been the slowest-ever in first-class cricket. After releasing one of his 'specials' Cranfield, like Barrie, followed the ball up the wicket. If the spin and swerve did not beat the batsman, he was ideally placed to block any scoring attempt with his leading boot, which by then would be hovering within a yard of the bat.

Harry Pilling, the diminutive Lancashire batsman of the 1970s, was extremely forthright about his bowling. Admittedly, he was rarely called upon to perform, and then only to entertain the crowd when there was no likelihood of a result.

On one occasion, when the umpire asked, for his own benefit and that of the batsman, what he was going to bowl, Pilling replied: 'Flighted filth, sir.'

When **Tom Goddard**, that fine servant of Gloucestershire, got his head down, even he had trouble in stopping himself. His career figures of 2,979 wickets – only four men have taken more – speak for themselves.

During one county match B.O. Allen, the Gloucestershire captain, was forced to leave the field and he handed the captaincy over to Goddard, who was bowling at the time. Over after over, Goddard continued to send down his steady brand of off-spin, although it was not a pitch for spinners. Finally, completely whacked, he turned to a colleague in the field and muttered:

'Why don't the bugger take me off?'

Goddard had bowled 42 consecutive overs in searing heat, and had forgotten that he was in charge of the team!

A veteran in his youth: Tom Goddard bowling for Gloucestershire against Surrey in 1934.

Uncommon pride in their work is a characteristic shared by many a fast bowler. Two who expressed their deepest feelings were Yorkshire's **Fred Trueman** and South Africa's **Peter Heine**.

Peter Parfitt, the Middlesex and England batsman, was relatively inexperienced on the day he faced up to Fiery Fred in a Championship match, tried to hook him, missed and took the ball full in the face.

It was a severe blow and Parfitt had to retire hurt. Nothing, fortunately, was broken, and Parfitt was able to resume his innings. On his return to the crease, Trueman showed unusual concern for the young Middlesex player. Later he revealed that he had said to him:

'When I hit 'em they usually don't come back.'

The Afrikaaner Heine shared Trueman's attitude. An uncompromising competitor for many years, he threatened to give up cricket the day he felled a batsman with a bouncer, walked up to the prostrate opponent, peered down at him and was not at all impressed.

'No blood?' said Heine. 'I must be getting old.'

Peter Heine is rigid with agony after Peter May has escaped narrowly in the Johannesburg Test in 1956 – 57.

If all the world's cricket clubs were invited to send in candidates for a Funny Run-Up Competition, the field would be large indeed. It is also interesting to note that not all approaches to the wicket are the innocent accidents of fate which they may seem.

Hugh Tayfield, South Africa's most successful slow bowler, would preface his run-up by tapping the turf a few times with the toe of each boot. This mannerism drove one or two inexperienced batsmen wild with anger and impatience – and it probably brought Tayfield a few wickets.

More explosive – or delayed-explosive – was the action of **Billy Chapman**, who played for many years for the village of Reighton in Yorkshire. He was a farmer, both wholehearted and fit, and capable of long spells of sustained fast bowling. He began his run-up twenty yards from the wicket, gathering pace as he went but in the last couple of strides braking suddenly so that on arrival at the crease he had come to a complete halt. He then drew back his arm and fired the ball up the pitch with all his strength.

It may have looked odd, but it worked for Billy who turned in some remarkable figures including 8 for 2 and 6 for 1. Though pleased with the results he brought them, several of Billy's clubmates tried to coach him out of his eccentric action; but Billy, a quiet man, just grinned and said nothing.

Weirdest of the weird was an **opening bowler for Plympton 2nd XI** in the Devon Coca Cola village league. At the far end of his fifteen-yard run he began by throwing out his left arm behind him, then ran two paces forward and stooped in a knees-bend. Straightening up, he ran two more paces and turned a complete circle using tiny, twittering steps. When he was once more facing the batsman, he zig-zagged towards the bowling crease and delivered the ball at medium pace. He was noted for his accuracy.

When asked about his run-up ritual, he explained that he was taught to bowl by his grandfather in a backyard measuring almost

Hopping glad: Hugh Tayfield snares another victim.

The eccentric rhythms of Tony Lock, floating up to the
wicket in 1958.

exactly twenty-two yards. In order to make room for a run-up, he had to start in the potting-shed. He pushed himself off the shed wall, ducked under the washing line, circled a tub of flowers and then slalomed past a row of flower-pots to the delivery point.

This method had served him well over the years and he claimed that if he disturbed his run-up pattern his bowling went to pieces.

More than one good bowler has, in fact, found his rhythm destroyed as a result of 'losing' his run-up, amongst them the Kent and Northamptonshire bowler John Dye, and, more recently, **Philippe Edmonds** of Middlesex and England who developed a stutter in his normally fluid run-up. Edmonds is something of an eccentric, a mischievous streak in him sometimes alienating captains and managers. A slow bowler, he once bowled a bouncer in a Test match and was warned by the umpire not to intimidate the batsman. He promptly bowled another bouncer.

His suspension from a Middlesex match in 1984 came about partly because, at a tense moment in play, he had preferred to lie flat on the ground in the outfield. Later, during a boring Test in Calcutta, it was entirely in

character for him to pick up a newspaper in the field and start to read it.

One of the most eccentric actions in Test cricket belonged to the Pakistani fast bowler **Asif Masood** (once, in error, called Massif Arsood by Brian Johnston) who performed a backward chassis like a ballroom dancer before starting his run-up. John Arlott said that when going forwards he looked like Groucho Marx chasing a pretty waitress.

In the first-class game it is now rare to find a true rabbit – a bowler or wicket-keeper who is hopeless at batting. A contender for Best of Breed in the 1920s and '30s was Leicestershire's **Haydon Smith,** who also suffered from a nervous stutter. At Trent Bridge one day he arrived at the wicket to face Harold Larwood. The first delivery came down and he managed to play it along the ground to Sam Staples at second slip. He promptly set off for the pavilion.

'Hey, come back,' called Staples, 'I didn't catch it.'

'You b-b-bloody liar,' said Smith, turning round but not stopping, 'you kn-kn-know you did.'

Nerves were also the problem of **W.D. Hamilton**, who won a Blue for Oxford in 1882. He scored 9 and 0 in the Varsity match, and might have had more except that after one stroke he set off in the wrong direction.

By Australian Test standards, fast bowler **Bill Johnston** was definitely one of Nature's Number Elevens. Then in 1953 he finished the tour of England with cricket's most eccentric batting average: 102.00. He played 17 innings on the tour, but was dismissed only once, by Vic Cannings in the match against Hampshire. In those innings he amassed 102 runs, hence his amazing average. Only two other players have finished the English season with an average in excess of 100, and their names are Bradman and Boycott.

Bill Johnston claims two souvenir stumps after an Australian Test victory in which he took 4 for 26 in England's second innings. Note the eccentric behaviour of the crowd, who have all remained in their seats.

Specialist in motor racing not cricket – Jim Clark, the world champion, offers a tempting delivery in a charity match against Lord Brabourne's XI at Mersham, Kent in 1966.

More rumblings from the lower orders occurred at Hove in 1911. The eccentric responsible was **Charles Alletson**, a normally dour performer who belied his reputation by hitting a sprightly 50 in an hour before lunch. He began the afternoon session by scoring his next 50 in 15 minutes, and in the following 15 minutes added 89 more, while the last man scored 10 not out.

Whatever had inspired him, no-one knows. Alletson's next highest score after the Hove match was 11, and then he was dropped by the county.

Shortage of energy rather than batting ability was the greatest problem for **Len Stamps**, groundsman and caretaker at St Michael's Worcestershire. He was a fine striker of the ball but, being more than a shade overweight, his speciality became boundaries rather than singles. Twos and threes he viewed with real disfavour. No ground was big enough to give him the opportunity of running four, even if he had been prepared to take it.

As league cricket became established, captains grew more adept at setting defensive fields and cutting off boundaries. In a match against Bromyard, Stamps hit 88, but 84 of them were scored in singles. At the end of his innings he was so drained he was incapable of fielding. He was taken home and detained in bed for two days with exhaustion. He was off work for a week until he had fully recovered.

Jemmy Shaw, the Notts fast bowler of the 1870s, was famed for his poor batting and was the undisputed No 11 in the county side. He was also noted for his wayward private life, and once a newspaper commented: 'The Notts No 11 did not go to bed at an orthodox hour.'

One night at Clifton, after a heavy drinking session, he failed to return to the team's hotel and was still missing the next day. Notts had one wicket left and needed 43 to avoid a follow-on. Thus Jemmy was due at the wicket when play resumed, partnered by his captain, Richard Daft.

As he entered the ground that morning, Daft fully expected to have to follow-on immediately since he was a man short. However, a Gloucestershire official informed him that his No 11 had been found asleep, or unconscious, under a tree on the Downs. Jemmy was rushed to the ground and his team-mates worked rapidly to restore his circulation, wash, clothe and generally wake him up. He was ready to walk to the wicket with just seconds to spare; Daft, at this stage,

said nothing.

Play began and Daft did his best to farm the bowling, though he could not manage to take every ball. At the other end Jemmy offered a series of grotesque strokes but somehow survived. They knocked off the runs required to save the follow-on, and when Jemmy was at last out he had made 9, his captain 92 not out. As they returned to the pavilion, Jemmy braced himself for the telling-off he knew must come.

'Jemmy,' said Daft sternly, 'I have a word of advice for you. I have never seen you play so well before. I suggest you waste no more money on hotel beds and sleep out in the open air for the rest of the season.'

In the eyes of the old **Nawab of Pataudi**, fielding was a dismal chore. Even as captain of India he did not disguise his disdain for aspects of play other than batting. The former captain of the Indian Gymkhana Club, C.M. Masters, confirmed that on four separate occasions the Nawab had scored a century before lunch, then reappeared in the afternoon with a doctor's certificate stating that he was unfit to field.

The **Reverend David Sheppard** was selected for the tour to Australia in 1962–63. His clerical duties had meant that he had not played much cricket for Sussex or England in the period prior to departure, and he knew he would be a little rusty. From the outset, Sheppard's slip fielding presented problems.

Fred Trueman, one of the most eccentric of all the great Yorkshire cricketers, was thus presented with a ready-made straight man and did not waste any chances. When another slip catch evaded Sheppard, he blustered:

'You might keep yer eye shut when yer prayin', Vicar, but I wish you'd keep 'em open when I'm bowlin'.'

In Western Australia a team party was attended by the Bishop of Perth. As he approached Sheppard, Trueman dug him in the ribs and said out of the corner of his mouth:

'Watch it, David, 'ere comes Senior Professional.'

During the match against Victoria, Bill Lawry, the Test opener, pulled a ball to leg and Sheppard ran round the boundary and held a superb catch. In his delight and relief at ending his drought, he hurled the ball high in the air. Unfortunately, he had failed to hear the umpire call no-ball. Meanwhile Lawry and

his partner pinched an extra run.

Sheppard did eventually take an authentic catch, whereupon Trueman remarked: 'When the Reverend puts his hands together, he's got a better chance than most of us.'

Warwick Armstrong was a rugged cricketer at the best of times, but his anger knew no bounds during the touring Australians' match against Kent in 1921. Leslie Troughton, the Kent captain, was a notoriously bad fielder, and when he managed both to stop the ball *and* run out Armstrong with his throw, the beefy Australian captain was at first dumbfounded then extremely cross. He flung his bat away and stumped off to the pavilion without it. There he ordered one of his team to go out and fetch the bat. Not wishing to offend the purple mammoth any more, the man did as he was told.

In 1919, the fielder-who-could-not-wait-to-clear-off-home was undoubtedly Yorkshire 12th man, **A.C. Williams**. In the match against Leicestershire at Huddersfield he was asked to act as substitute for the visitors, and caught out four of his own side.

A **newcomer to a London club** was placed at mid-on. It was a hot afternoon, not ideal for a concentrated spell in the field. The newcomer was soon called into action, but regrettably failed to answer the call and the ball sped past him to the boundary; he, meanwhile, was busy chasing and trying to catch a butterfly. The next ball went past him as he bent to tie his shoelace. He was moved to square-leg where the ball again went past him as he posed for a photograph for two American tourists. Two deliveries later he was

hit on the back by the ball after he had turned to wave goodbye to his American friends.

At the end of the over he asked the captain when it would be his turn to bowl. The reply was unprintable.

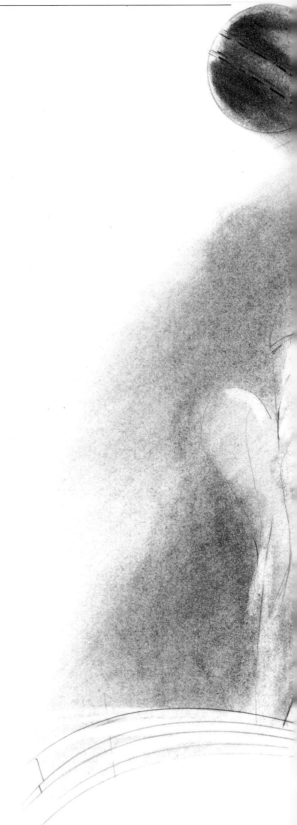

Larger than life:
Warwick
Armstrong.

Now to wicket-keepers. Many are known to nurture fantasies of being demon bowlers, but should they be allowed to try? They will say that from their unique vantage-point they know more about bowling than bowlers, but there is a slight difference between knowing and doing.

At one time it did seem as though the **Honourable Alfred Lyttelton** had delivered the goods. This was at the Oval Test in 1884, the first time that all eleven players had bowled in a Test match, The Australians were going well when W.G. Grace put on the pads

The Honourable Alfred Lyttelton – wicket-keeper/bowler.

while the England captain, Lord Harris, gave wicket-keeper Lyttelton a chance with his lobs. He bowled 12 overs and took 4 for 19 as Australia were eventually dismissed for 551. On several occasions subsequently the experiment was given further try-outs, but with nothing like the success of that first attempt.

Herbert Strudwick knew in his heart that a wicket-keeper's place was behind the stumps. His county record shows that he did bowl once or twice for Surrey, taking 0 for 60 in the course of a 22-year career. But wicket-keeping was the thing, and 'Struddy' placed particular value on hardening his hands; to this end he would regularly soak them in the chamber-pot.

Keith Miller had a notably less serious attitude. When, as captain of New South Wales, he led his team out on to the field at

ALBANIAN STARS?

C.B.FRY

Sydney, someone on the Hill informed him that there were 11 men tailing behind him. The team refused Miller's first solution of 'Which one of you will get lost?' Instead they opted for seniority, the youngest to leave. The youngest was the wicket-keeper. So Miller, at that time the world's best all-rounder, went behind the stumps.

Keith Miller, centre, always an elegant figure.

Miller has been described by the former Australian captain Richie Benaud as the most enterprising captain he played under. Miller's method of setting his well-drilled New South Wales team in the field was simply to say, when they got to the middle: 'OK, fellas, scatter.'

Perhaps the greatest all-round all-rounder was **Charles Burgess Fry,** who captained England in six Tests between 1912 and 1920. England were unbeaten during that time. Fry scored more than 39,000 first-class runs with a career average of over 50.

He also played other sports. He was the world long-jump record-holder for 25 years. He gained two caps for the England football team and played in the 1902 Cup Final for Southampton. He played rugby for the Barbarians – and would probably have won an England rugby cap if he had not had to drop out of the University match 10 days before the game. He was also a county-standard tennis player and golfer. He was offered the throne of Albania, but declined. His book is called *A Life Worth Living.*

Hanif Mohammad, the holder of the record individual innings of 499, was an eccentric of a different kind, who delighted in slowly grinding his opponents into the dust during his many long, remorseless innings, throughout which he would neither by movement nor by expression reveal the slightest trace of emotion.

If, on the other hand, he bowled, it was mainly for entertainment. Playing for Pakistan against Somerset in 1954, Hanif twice came on for a single over. Each time he bowled a remarkable mixture of four right-handed deliveries and two left-handed.

Graham Gooch is a man of so many talents that it is difficult to select one area in which he shines most brightly. Some critics say that he so strikingly resembles a sergeant-major in Queen Victoria's Army, he should be in films, not cricket. He has also been known to keep a straight face in the Essex dressing-room. For a time in the early 1980s it seemed that only his brilliant batting could lift England out of her doldrums. But he was banned from Test matches for going on a tour to South Africa, and county attacks suffered against Essex while bowlers prospered against England, who also missed his bowling – right-arm medium pace, when serious, sometimes becoming slow left-arm, or fast right-arm in the famous impersonation of Bob Willis in full cry.

The man's multiple abilities were apparent in Calcutta during the Fourth Test against India in 1982. Gooch batted with supreme authority to score 153. He bowled right- and left-handed in the same Indian innings. On the rest day he went to the local golf course and recorded a hole in one.

HATTRICK!
1 BATMAN HAT   2 BOWLER HAT   3 GOLF HANDI-CAP!

UMPIRICAL CHORDS

The best-remembered umpires all seem to have had a special way of dealing with those epic confrontations that are bound to occur when great players meet and the margin between success and error is so slight. Humour often plays a part, serving as an oblique reminder that it is only a game after all – even though no-one seems to think so at the time.

Frank Chester recalled a clash between two of England's greatest cricketers, Harold Larwood and Wilfred Rhodes. Larwood had been taking some hammer from the Yorkshire batsmen, and when Rhodes came in to bat his habit of sticking out his left foot touched a raw spot with the Nottinghamshire paceman, and he muttered to Umpire Chester that he would flatten it.

Down came the next ball, right on target. Rhodes leapt in agony and hopped about shaking his wounded toes. Chester gave him a couple of minutes and then, as he was about to resume his innings, inquired:

'Are you all right, Wilfred?'

'Aye.'

'Can you walk?'

'Aye.'

'Well, you can walk to the pavilion. You were lbw!'

Not all umpires are so generous. **Frank Lee** had a certain reputation as a hard man, especially when it came to giving lbw decisions. **Eric Hollies,** the Warwickshire and England spinner, was one of several who felt that Lee's umpiring would be improved if he would only dismiss a few batsmen. One April evening, Hollies was seated close to Lee at a start-of-season cricket dinner. He noticed the umpire wagging his finger about to emphasize a point, and called out:

'That's right, Frank, wag it about now all you want, then put it away until September!'

Lee had an amusing clash with **Wilf Wooller,** Welsh rugby international, inspiring captain of Glamorgan and a man who has always spoken his mind fearlessly. When

Frank Chester and the arts of communication.

Frank Lee, left, on duty with the imposing figure of Syd
Buller alongside.

Leicestershire were batting in a match against Glamorgan, Lee turned down an appeal for leg-before. At the end of the over Wooller, who had been fielding at wide mid-off, came up to Lee and said:

'Frank, that was a bad decision. I could see he was out from where I was standing.'

Later, when Glamorgan were batting, Wooller came in and asked for guard. Lee, standing over the stumps, asked: 'Where will you have it from, Wilf? Here?' Then he walked over to wide mid-off. 'Or from here?'

Arthur Fagg was another umpire who stood no nonsense from players, whatever their reputation. He refused to stand for the first over of the morning in a Test at Edgbaston in 1973 because the West Indian team had made such a fuss after he had given Geoff Boycott not out. In another match, when Australian captain Bill Lawry bitterly requested why he had been given out, Fagg coolly replied: 'Lbw.'

'Lbw?' said Lawry in disgust, 'but I hit the bloody ball.'

'I know,' said Fagg. 'That's why you were given out caught behind.'

In his playing days for Kent Fagg had a similarly blunt tongue. A huge bumble bee was flying around the head of an opposing batsman during a long stand on a hot day.

'What should I do with it?' asked the batsman. Fagg's reply was politer than it might have been.

'Catch it and put it on a length,' said Arthur, 'none of our bowlers will get near it.'

Alec Skelding, the former Leicestershire bowler, was a firm believer in the power of humour and used it on many an occasion when he became an umpire. His technique for defusing the tension after an impossibly close run-out appeal was to wait for the yells of the fielding side to die down, then say:

'Gentlemen, it's a photo-finish. But as I have neither the time nor the equipment, the batsman is not out.'

After he retired from playing, Skelding acted for some time as scorer for his county. One day when the scoring had been particularly heavy, there was a difference of opinion in the scorebox over the correct total at close of play. Crowds of people gathered outside the box, demanding to be told the correct official score. As the tumult grew louder, and the prospect of a settlement seemed no closer, Skelding stuck his head out of the scorebox and beckoned a small boy

Alec Skelding of Leicestershire, a master of the defusing phrase.

from the crowd. He pressed a penny into the boy's hand and said:

'Go and buy an evening paper. We'll get it from that.'

Beyond the confines of county cricket, free from the scrutiny of the press corps and television cameras, one or two eccentric umpires have been known to not-exactly-bend-the-rules. This is not to be confused with cheating, in order to favour one team over the other, or even with hiding a mistake to avoid personal embarrassment. Not-exactly-bending-the-rules is more a matter of reinterpreting them in the light of some deeply held conviction.

On the Bristol and District circuit, **George Humphreys** was a well-known character. He first played for a club connected with a well-known Christian movement, but after one match he and three team-mates heavily contravened the club rules about temperance and were obliged to resign. George went off and joined Stapleton.

He enjoyed a splendid club career, but one point of law irritated him enormously – that which allowed him to be given out lbw while sweeping. On his retirement from playing he quietly set about repairing this 'injustice', to such good effect that when in his mid-sixties he retired from umpiring he could claim to have turned down about 5,000 such appeals!

Umpirical discord threatened to spoil a match played on King George V's Jubilee Day in 1935. It had been arranged by Lord Dorchester between Greywell, his local village in Hampshire, and the Old Optimists, for whom **Syd Levey** was a prominent performer.

The match got off to a controversial start, thanks to the local umpire who by lunchtime had unkindly returned seven Optimists batsmen to the pavilion. At the interval Syd decided to have a chat with the umpire. Looking out across the field, he ventured a remark about the spire of the parish church, saying it must be all of 200 feet high.

'Nonsense,' said the umpire, 'it's less than 100 feet.'

Neither man was prepared to give in to the other's view and a bet of five shillings was struck. However, in the Laws of Cricket, as revised in 1931, no umpire was allowed to take part in wagers (Law 51). Law 52 stated that an umpire could be dismissed if he flouted Law 51. The Greywell umpire was dismissed, and the match continued in a far more agreeable atmosphere.

Urgent diplomacy was called for in the match at Arundel between the home team, led by the **Duke of Norfolk**, and Sussex

Martlets. The Duke was at the non-striker's end when his partner decided it was time to give His Grace and captain a turn at batting. He played a ball into the covers and set off for what should have been a comfortable single. The Duke also ran, but stumbled in mid-pitch and was still trying to disentangle pads, feet and bat when the stumps were broken. It now fell to the umpire to answer the Martlets' appeals for a dismissal. The umpire was Mr Meadows, the Duke's butler, and he, caught between loyalty and the truth, uttered the famous verdict: 'His Grace is not in.'

More down-to-earth was the umpire in the Mod-Dec Devon Cricket League who had a devastating answer to bowlers making frivolous appeals. In his coat he concealed a device which gave out shrieks of hysterical laughter, audible right round the ground.

Still more down-to-earth was the special equipment which awaited visiting umpires to the Sussex village of Northchapel in the 1940s and '50s. Instead of pebbles for counting the number of balls in an over, they were presented with a set of rabbit droppings.

Northchapel umpires always counted with them, the visitors would be told. 'They're nice and hard, sir, and not as heavy as pebbles.'

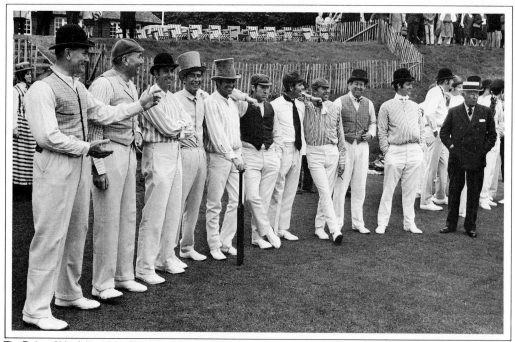

The Duke of Norfolk with his Eleven before a charity match 'in the 1870s style' against Sussex in 1971. On the left are the Bedser twins, Alec and Eric.

When Sarfraz Nawaz broke his bat during the third Test v England at Lahore in 1984, the umpire was presented with a special 'shortie', and promptly offered it to the batsman.

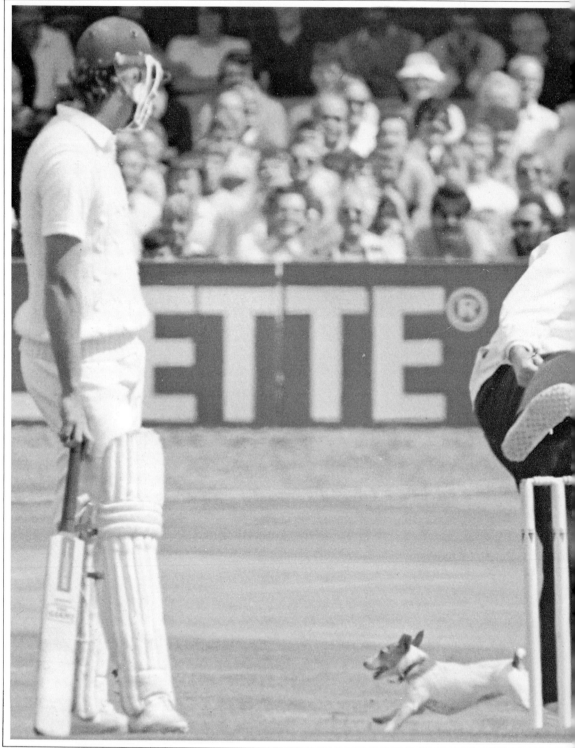

At Headingley in 1984, umpire David Constant invents a
new signal: Dog Invasion!

THE IMPORTANCE OF TEA

Players, umpires and spectators alike are united in their need for a cup of mid-afternoon tea. If **Arthur Shrewsbury,** the Notts and England batsman, had to bat after lunch, he always asked the pavilion attendant to make sure and bring him a cup of tea at exactly half-past four.

Test umpires **David Constant** and **Alan Whitehead** refused to leave the field during the tea interval of Hampshire's John Player League match with Essex in 1984. They sat on the square as a way of making the point that a reduction in the tea interval to just fifteen minutes made it impossible for them to get and drink a cup of tea, quite apart from anything else they might wish to do.

On the day of their protest, tea was taken out to the umpires.

At Taunton in 1946, on the third day of a county game, a wicket fell and the fielding side waited for the next batsman to appear. To their amazement, instead of a batsman, **a lady with an umbrella** and a huge picnic basket appeared down the pavilion steps. She walked straight through the fielders, and calmly disappeared into the crowd.

The mystery was later solved. On the first two days she had brought her husband's tea and crossed the ground while the official tea interval was still in progress. On the third day, the tea interval is at a different time.

The importance of champagne. Jack Hobbs toasts the crowd after completing his 126th first-class century.

ONLY HUMAN NATURE

Many strange acts are committed on the cricket field which may seem eccentric to the casual spectator, though to the players who commit them they are quite understandable if not perfectly natural. They are cricket's equivalent of the *crime passionel,* done in the heat of the moment and defended, or otherwise, at leisure.

As the old timers used to say: '**W.G. Grace** never actually broke the rules, but it was amazing what he could do with them'. The Doctor's competitive spirit drove him to what others might call extremes. He, on the other hand, had his public to think of. 'They've come to see me bat, not you umpiring', he told one official who gave W.G. out before he felt his time was due – so he replaced the bails and continued with his innings.

Cricket's most famous face.

'When you win the toss, bat'. That was Grace's firm belief. If the weather or the wicket suggested otherwise, he had an alternative dictum: 'If in doubt, consult your team-mates, then bat.' After all, the Doctor himself feared no bowler, in any conditions.

All Grace anecdotes, to be appreciated, have to take into account not only his reputation as the 'Champion' cricketer, but also his huge frame and, by contrast, his curiously high-pitched voice. Some stories which have attached themselves to this classic cricket eccentric may have become a little exaggerated or confused over the years, but here are a few further reported highlights from the career of the 'great law-maker'.

While playing for Gloucestershire against Surrey in 1878, W.G. was running between the wickets when the ball was thrown in and lodged in the ample folds of his shirt. Having taken three runs already, he profited from this chance possession of the ball to run three more until the Surrey fielders blocked his path and stopped him. Harry Jupp demanded that the Doctor give up the ball, but he refused to do so for fear that the Surrey players would have him dismissed for 'handling the ball'. The dispute lasted several minutes and was resolved only by consulting the umpires, who declared that Grace was not out and that three runs should be counted.

Grace was doubly stuck at Clifton on another occasion. First he was stuck for runs against a difficult off-break bowler. In one over he fenced at the first five balls with no success, then lashed at the sixth with a hook shot. Unfortunately he got a bottom edge and the ball dropped into the top of one of his pads and stuck there. While those around him goggled, the Doctor waddled to the boundary with ball in pad, crossed the line and demanded four runs. To his obvious disgust the umpire made no gesture.

He had better luck with the umpire on the day he made a towering hit into the outfield during a county match. While on his second run, he could see that a fielder had arrived under the ball, so he immediately declared the innings closed. He was also pleased with his next move, which was to browbeat the umpire into giving him not out on the grounds that the ball was caught after his declaration.

W.G. pulled off another surprise declaration in an 1893 match, suddenly declaring the innings closed with his own score on 93. When asked why, he replied that it was the only score between 0 and 100 that

he had not made.

W.G. Grace was also responsible for cricket's first hijack. The 'victim' was William Midwinter, an Australian batsman whom Grace had first spotted playing for Victoria in 1874. Three years later Midwinter came over to play for Gloucestershire.

The following year Midwinter joined the touring Australian party, and on 20 June he and Charles Bannerman went out to bat for the tourists against Middlesex at Lord's. Meanwhile, across the river, Gloucestershire were playing Surrey, and Grace formulated a

The greatest eccentric of them all.

dastardly plan that Conan Doyle would have been proud of. He and J.A. Bush hired a taxi, drove to Lord's and hijacked Midwinter to play for Gloucestershire again.

The Australians were greatly incensed, and the row went on until W.G. sent them a letter apologizing for the escapade, and the fact that 'in the heat of the moment I used unparliamentary language'.

In Memoriam: two stories concerning busts of W.G. The more unusual one was presented to Lord's in 1969. It was made by Mr Vic Wilson, a Leeds bus driver who spurned conventional materials and somehow modelled the great man in matchsticks – 12,454 of them.

The second had stood in the Long Room for as long as either of the two oldest MCC members could remember. One day in 1939 they were staggered to see it being moved, and in Neville Cardus's time-honoured story, one member turned to the other and remarked sombrely:

'This means war.'

Mention of Lord's recalls another apocalyptic statement, recorded in a letter to *The Times* of 25 June 1968:

'Sir,
Now I know this country is finished. On Saturday, with Australia playing, I asked a London cabby to take me to Lord's. I had to show him the way.
Your obedient servant
D.M. Brittain'

Another member of the Grace family who would stand no nonsense from umpires was W.G.'s elder brother, **E.M.**, the coroner. Here he describes an over he bowled for Thornbury against Weston-super-Mare:

'F.L. Cole made one off my first ball, F.A. Leeston Smith six off my second, six off the third, six off the fourth and six off the fifth. The umpire then said it was over. "No it isn't," I said. "Shut up, I am going to have another." And off this one he was stumped!'

By then E.M. had for many years upheld the family tradition for eccentricity. As a schoolboy in Long Ashton, he was once given out lbw. He disagreed with the decision and left the field with the stumps under his arm.

Australia's answer to 'W.G.' – Kevin McEvoy of the Western Australia Institute of Technology tries an impression of the great man.

Eccentricity – or rampant ambition? Before deciding, readers may like to put themselves in the position of Kent bowler **George Collins**. At Dover in 1922 he had taken all nine of the Notts wickets to fall. 'Tich' Freeman was bowling at the other end. The ball was edged to Collins at slip. . . and he deliberately dropped it. In the following over he took his tenth wicket.

Not cricket, perhaps. But Collins, no doubt, was more than eager to make his mark. It must have been a tough life working in the shadow of Freeman, and the prospect of becoming only the second Kent bowler after Colin Blythe to take ten wickets in an innings seems to have eclipsed his sense of duty to the county.

For another former Kent player, it was fatherly pride which sent him the wrong way. **Colin Cowdrey** was driving to work on 29 November 1984. Listening to the car radio, he was immersed in the ball-by-ball commentary of the First Test in India. When his son Christopher came on to bowl his first over in Test cricket, father's thoughts became so firmly fixed on the Sub-Continent that he turned his car the wrong way up a one-way street.

Flagged down by an amazed policeman, Colin was trying to explain his behaviour when, with his fourth ball, Christopher bowled Kapil Dev for 42. Father got off with a caution.

Colin Cowdrey still in some doubt about the right direction.

77

Not all English cricketers regard the first-class county game as the be-all and end-all of their lives. **Cecil Parkin,** for example was perfectly happy in league cricket, though there may be a good reason for this. As a young man Parkin played one game for Yorkshire, in 1906. It was then discovered that he had been born twenty yards outside the county boundary, and he was quickly released. Parkin turned to league cricket until Lancashire signed him in 1914 and he stayed with them until 1926. To have played for each of the Roses counties is a truly remarkable feat, but to have done so after such a disorienting start in life is even more commendable.

Parkin, for all that, was a permanently wayward figure. On the 1920–21 tour to Australia he was openly critical of his captain's bowling:

'Go on, Mr Douglas,' said Cecil, 'you bowl 'em in, and after tea I'll bowl 'em out.'

He also tried to persuade his captain to bowl from the scoreboard end. 'Yes,' he said, 'you can see your analysis from there.'

S. F. BARNES (STAFFORDSHIRE).

Sydney Barnes was another with a liking for league cricket, and the minor counties circuit. Despite taking 189 wickets for England at 16.43 runs each in 27 Tests, he played in fewer than 100 first-class matches in a 35-year career. Perhaps he preferred the relative calm of Staffordshire to the hubbub of Lancashire, or, simply, chose to play the game on his own terms, with no meddling from

Cecil Parkin – a problem from birth.

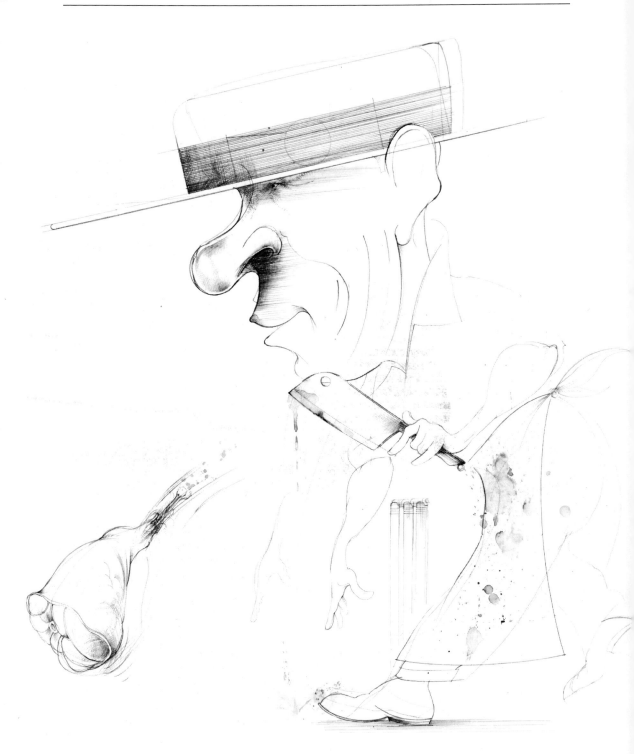

committees. Barnes of the four-square figure, huge hands and fierce, cadaverous features, was completely his own man, independent to the point of stubbornness: an eccentric of a different kind.

League cricket has a considerable reputation for toughness, and for tactics that might be thought ungentlemanly outside the Northern orbit. In 1964 **Rishton** played Burnley in the final of the Worsley (now Martini) Cup. Burnley had the feared West Indies fast bowler Charlie Griffith playing for them. Rishton, the underdogs, entered their dressing-room to find a bottle of fruit salts, courtesy of the opposition! Rishton, suitably effervesced, ran out and won.

The confidence of **Arthur Mailey** took a battering as he ground away for New South Wales with his leg-breaks and googlies while Victoria notched up their world record innings of 1,107. Arthur, however, had an excuse. Turning in figures of 4 for 362, he said they had been ruined by an idiot sitting in the Members' Stand in a cap and raincoat, who had dropped four catches off his bowling!

It was a typical remark by Mailey, an amusing character who delighted in drawing caricatures of his fellow cricketers and who entitled his autobiography *10 For 66 And All That*, after his most famous bowling analysis. On retirement, after a spell in journalism, he became a butcher in Cronulla, and scrawled on his window:

'I bowled tripe, I wrote tripe, and now I am selling it.'

Just as George Collins, the Kent bowler, had been determined to get his tenth wicket, so Lancashire's **Alan Wharton,** on 99, was determined that nothing should go wrong. His main problem, as he saw it, was his partner Cyril Washbrook, with whom he did not always see eye to eye.

Washbrook, with 90 to his credit, had strike. He pushed the ball to mid-wicket and set off for a quick single. Wharton refused to budge, forcing Washbrook to put on all brakes and turn tail. In a cloud of dust he just made his ground. Rising to his feet, his shirt and trousers newly daubed with green and brown patches, he turned to his partner and sternly said:

'It is a well-known fact that I am the best judge of a single in the country'.

Wharton replied: 'And it's a well-known fact that when I'm on 99 I am the best judge of a single in the whole bloody world!'

In the Third Test at Melbourne in 1937, the eagerness of that dynamic cricketer **Walter Robins** to compensate for a first-innings duck led to a sudden fit of eccentric running. Only minutes before stumps on the fifth day England, set 689 to win, were still 534 runs adrift with four wickets down. Robins came out to join **Maurice Leyland,** who had battled through a long hot day.

Maurice Leyland of the tired legs.

Robins managed to play O'Reilly's first ball through the gulley, set off like a whippet and came back for a second. The way seemed clear, so he sprinted off for a third, only to find that he had lapped Leyland! Robins quickly turned back and made his ground, then advanced to make his apologies.

'Take it easy,' gasped the weary Leyland, 'we can't make all those runs tonight!'

Self-preservation was undoubtedly the motive behind **Wally Hardinge's** actions one day at Canterbury. G.J. Bryan was taking a

WILLS'S CIGARETTES
No 19
CRICKETERS, 1928
A SERIES OF 50

H. T. W. HARDINGE
(KENT).

A product of the Kent nursery at Tonbridge, Hardinge appeared first for his county in 1902, becoming a regular member of the eleven five years later. At the age of 42 he is still a reliable right-handed first-wicket batsman and a useful slow left-hand bowler. An innings of 249 not out against Leicestershire in 1922, is the highest of his 63 three-figure scores, while he has four times made more than 2,000 runs in a season, and on four occasions put together two centuries in a match. He played once for England against Australia—at Leeds in 1921—and has represented his country at Soccer.

W. D. & H. O. WILLS
ISSUED BY THE IMPERIAL TOBACCO CO. (OF GREAT BRITAIN & IRELAND), LTD.

CONSTABLE REPRINT

walk behind the pavilion when he spotted Hardinge, senior pro, double international and astute businessman, climbing out of the dressing-room window.

'What on earth are you doing?' asked Bryan.

As he jumped from the window, Hardinge replied: 'I've run myself out, and his Lordship (Lord Harris) is on his way round here!'

On-field mannerisms seem to have multiplied with the advent of the one-day game. There is prize money to be had, cups and medals and instant fame via television, and usually more things happen per ball than in the two-innings game. As a means of relieving their tensions, players often go in more than wholeheartedly for punching the air with fist and bat, for Caribbean handslaps, intimidatory appeals,

ungentlemanly signals, shameless necking, and so forth. Meanwhile, patient wives video the whole performance so that the old man will have something to look forward to in retirement.

The pace of one-day cricket, and its show-business elements, would have surprised even an old-time rebel like South African **Eric Rowan,** who regularly had problems with officialdom. In 1949, for example, he was hauled before the South African Board for giving a V-sign on the field. Rowan offered the defence that it was really a Churchillian salute. When a Board member disagreed, Rowan replied:

'Well, it depends on which side of the

Eric Rowan plays a shot to appease the South African Board.

field you are.'

An arguable point, just, and reminiscent of those gentler days when **Charlie Harris**, the Notts opening bat, used to greet the fielding side with the words: 'Good morning, fellow workers.' He also on occasion liked to hang a sign reading 'Do Not Disturb' over the bails.

Cricketers have always been successful in adapting to circumstances. In the 1840s, when scoreboards were in their extreme infancy, players had to keep their own up-to-the-minute accounts. **Nicholas Felix**, the Kent and England batsman, used to keep his own score by marking up runs on his starched shirt front.

We have encountered some of the game's ambidextrous bowlers in another chapter ('Specialists in their Art'). Batsmen with two front feet are a still rarer breed, but when Somerset were playing Notts in 1930 batsman **George Hunt** clutched gladly at the idea as it floated through his mind. He was having severe problems with Voce's inswingers, and so he decided to bat left-handed against Voce and right-handed against the rest of the Notts attack. It worked – for a while.

Lord Lionel Tennyson's problem was not how to keep his man at the wicket but how to dislodge him. While captaining Hampshire against Middlesex at Lord's, he decided that Philip Mead was batting much too slowly. He wrote out a telegram and had it delivered to the batsman at the crease. 'Too slow', it read. 'Get out at once'.

In the early years of the nineteenth century, the wide ball was used without penalty as a tactic for driving batsmen into a frenzy of frustration, in which state they were more vulnerable to a sudden accurate delivery. **James Breadbridge** of Sussex decided to counter wides bowled to him by literally throwing his bat at the ball. He practised hard and achieved limited success with his tomahawk stroke. Its chief flaw was that the batsman had little control over directing the ball once he had made contact with it. Against England in 1827, he threw his bat as usual but was mortified to see the ball deflected into the hands of William Ward fielding at point!

Arthur Coningham, a member of the 1893 Australian side to England, showed an inventiveness which his contemporary, Lord Baden-Powell, would have admired. While fielding at Lord's on an exceptionally cold day, he gathered sticks and fallen branches from outside the boundary, and built and lit a fire to warm himself.

A Danish cricketer was so unhinged by being given out lbw first ball that he exacted a strange revenge. He stormed from the field in Copenhagen and immediately drove seventy miles home to Kalundborg. His team-mates would not have minded so much but the vehicle he used was the coach in which they had all travelled to the match that morning.

Another tale of motorized vengeance: batsmen from the Cornish village team of **Perranarworthal** were forced to run for their lives during a game with St Gluvius in June 1983. A minivan raced on to the St Gluvius ground, flattened both wickets and sped away. An hour later, the driver was spotted watching the game from behind a hedge, and was later interviewed by the police. The incident failed to stop Perranarworthal winning by one wicket.

As in Cornwall, so in Somerset cricket can excite reactions which non-cricketers might term eccentric. Before the days of league cricket, the neighbouring villages of Crowcombe and Stogumber had stirred up a long-standing feud. Stogumber complained bitterly that many umpiring decisions went against them, especially after 7 pm when the Crowcombe umpire, who was also the local publican, needed to open his hostelry. For their part, Crowcombe complained that a Stogumber farmer should not have allowed his cows to graze on the pitch after milking them at 4.30!

In 1968, **Dave Baker** of Crowcombe did the unforgiveable. He joined Stogumber and was refused a beer at the end of the match in the Crowcombe local. Dave soon found an effective solution. He was the local milkman, so the entire village of Crowcombe (pop. 660) went without milk the following day!

Cricket spectators should not be too censorious of the violent deeds they may see on the professional tennis circuit. Those highly paid entertainers will have their tantrums from time to time, but let no-one think that men such as John McEnroe or Jimmy Connors actually invented 'abuse' of their chosen instrument.

As far back as 1922, Hampshire's **George Brown** was extremely upset to be dropped down the batting order – and showed it. Coming in at No 10, he smashed a ball for six over the wicket-keeper's head. The blow split his bat, so he tore it in two, handed half the blade to the umpire and successfully batted on with the other half. A countryman of immense strength and courage, Brown used to pride himself on batting against fast bowling without gloves.

More recently **Majid Khan** was annoyed at his dismissal while playing for Glamorgan against Derbyshire. On his return to the pavilion Majid found a saw and did not rest until his bat lay in two pieces on the floor, now lightly coated with willow dust.

Eccentric? Possibly, but then some people will do anything for a laugh.

ECCENTRIC DRESSERS

Two pioneers of headgear for self-protection were **Richard Daft** of Notts, who in the 1870 often swathed his head in a towel, and **Patsy Hendren** of Middlesex. In 1933 Hendren took to wearing a kind of deerstalker. A contemporary report said this had the side-effect of converting his appearance from that of an amiable but hungry bull mastiff into that of an amiable but hungry bloodhound.

"CHUMS"
RICKETERS

—E. HENDREN

esex and England. A
and vigorous hitter, and
nd sportsman. Alert in
t. he was one of the main-
f the champion county in
oring 2,013 runs with av.
. Plays for Brentford
er.

(Photo: S. & G.)

these real photos by
ing "CHUMS"
at once

More spectacular was the arrival at the wicket of skydiver **Peter Ellis**. He planned to parachute on to the pitch at the start of the match in June 1969 between Temple Cloud and Harlech TV, and open the batting. Onlookers saw Ellis leap from the aircraft at 3,000 feet, then there was a brilliant blue flash as he bounced off an 11,000-volt electricity cable, stampeding a herd of cattle and cutting off the supply of current to seven surrounding villages. The collision also meant that Ellis missed the cricket pitch but he landed quite unhurt in the next field, marched to the wicket in his crash helmet and notched a score of 1 before he was dismissed.

Arthur Shrewsbury of Notts and England was probably the finest batsman of the 1880s and '90s after W.G. Grace. Team-mates never saw him without a hat and many were unaware that he was completely bald. He always wore a cap on the cricket field, and a bowler hat off it, and changed into a night-cap when he retired to bed. Legend has it that he took his bat with him to bed as well!

The story is well known of the legendary **Brown of Brighton** who bowled so fast that one of his deliveries beat the batsman, wicket-keeper and long-stop, ripped through a coat flung at it by a spectator, and killed a dog. Less well known is the reaction of the brave man, one **Little Dench**, who for many years after the famous incident fielded at long-stop to Brown. To guard against being fatally struck by a similar ball, the long-stop never took the field without a large wad of hay stuffed down his shirt.

R.G. Barlow, the Lancashire all-rounder, had some eccentric customers at his shop in Stretford Road, close to the Old Trafford ground, where he sold cricket mementoes and associated articles. In the days when Johnny Crossland, who allegedly bowled in a sweater because he had no shirt beneath it, was hurling down his thunderbolts for the county, a young man walked into the shop one morning.

'Do you sell sports equipment?' he asked.

'Of course,' Barlow replied.

'Then,' said the young man, 'give me a bottle of arnica, a court plaster and an arm-sling. I'm batting against Crossland this afternoon.'

Whoever first wrote that 'goalkeepers are barmy' would probably have said the same of wicket-keepers. The nature of their work demands enormous concentration and consistency, not to speak of regular gravity-defying leaps which eventually erode the elbows completely. Their captains also prefer them to suffer injury with stoicism, because a replacement 'keeper usually means a heavy toll of extras.

In a Test in Melbourne **George Duckworth**, of Lancashire and England, was suffering from a badly bruised hand. Rather than give up the gloves he resorted to an old remedy – a piece of beefsteak which he slipped over his wounded palm. This worked

Geoff Boycott in disguise on a dusty day in Port of Spain.

Moments of light relief for England cricketers on tour. An MCC party on the *SS Stratheden* bound for Australia in 1950, left to right, Trevor Bailey, Reg Simpson, Gilbert Parkhouse, Denis Compton, Arthur McIntyre and Len Hutton. Opposite: Mike Brearley, top left, and Chris Tavaré, top right, on Christmas Day 1981 in Delhi with, bottom right, Allan Lamb as the Pink Panther and Godfrey Evans, bottom left, doing his Carmen Miranda act on the *Edinburgh Castle* en route to South Africa, 1956.

reasonably well, but unfortunately the steak could not be replaced because the Melbourne butchers were shut for three days over a long weekend. By the second innings, the good news had been passed round the entire fly population of Victoria, and this severely hampered the 'keeper's field of vision. Duckworth was only consoled by the fact that the Australian batsmen were also forced to become actors in the farce, as the flies buzzed madly round in their search for putrescent steak.

Despite being selected seven times in the early 1920s to keep wicket for England, **George Brown** was prevented during this period from being first-choice 'keeper for Hampshire by W.H. Livsey, a stumper of some renown. When Livsey was absent from the county side, Brown was naturally asked to replace him – but did so reluctantly. To show his disdain for the position of reserve wicket-keeper, Brown, a motor-cycle enthusiast, always took the field in motor-cycle gauntlets. He became so used to wearing them in this

dual role, he even wore them while 'keeping for England!

Few wicket-keepers can have outdone **O. Creed** for quantity of equipment. His dressing ceremony was also something to behold. During the late 1940s he played for the University club in Wellington, New Zealand. He would arrive at the ground ten minutes before play. If his side were fielding, he would then station himself three paces outside the boundary at long-leg. Here he would begin to divest, having already ordered the nearest small boy to go off and wet his inners. From a huge bag he drew out a mass of cricket clothing and equipment. Starting with the athletic support, he put it all on, including several body protectors and two sets of leg-guards as well as up to four sweaters, topping it all off with a thick choker and an old, Australian-style cap.

So overloaded with kit was O. Creed that when he slipped one day, while taking a catch on the leg side, it took three men to lift him to his feet again.

Ten thousand people watching a charity game between the RAF and the Lord's Taverners at Cranwell on 5 May 1971 were amazed when one of the RAF team came to the wicket carrying a polo stick. It was **Prince Charles**. He scored 10 runs in as many minutes before being bowled by Ken Barrington. He gained his revenge by bowling Barrington and having Bill Edrich stumped. He took 2 for 37 in 7 overs, but the Taverners won with one ball remaining.

Australian tourists are usually not too complimentary about the weather in early summer in England. On the 1972 tour, **David Colley**, a fast bowler, played against Surrey at the Oval during May wearing a vest, a sweater, a shirt, then two more sweaters on top. The temperature was around 54°F.

David Colley, a very cold Australian.

Ronald Gregory, a slow bowler from Butterley, found that one of his boots was affecting his run-up during a Notts and Derbyshire Border League game. He gave the boot to an umpire, and at the end of the over changed into his everyday shoe. Wearing one cricket boot and one black shoe, he proceeded to take a hat-trick!

Five minutes before the end of the championship match at Worcester on 22 July 1954, **Roly Jenkins**, the England spin bowler, felt a nail protruding through his foot. He took off the offending boot, then the other one, and bowled the remaining four balls in his socks.

A fast bowler in the Cheshire League was told by his captain that he would be dropped if he persisted in wearing plimsolls instead of cricket boots. He turned up the following week with new boots but no kit. On being questioned, he revealed that he had been staying with his sister, who had burnt his kit. Why? Because he had failed to repay the money she had lent him to buy the boots!

A club player developed a cunning ploy in the field (or so he thought). He always wore his sweater back to front, claiming that it confused the batsmen!

Ossie Wheatley's demanding social life was responsible for his arriving one day at Colchester to captain Glamorgan – still clad in the dinner jacket he had worn to a club dinner in London the previous evening. He was glad to win the toss and then sat back and watched his team score 322 for 7 – one of their better efforts that year.

Ossie Wheatley, never at his most elegant with a bat.

Leslie Todd went out to field at third man for Kent at the start of a championship match. In the first over he sprinted to try and cut off a fierce shot but, realizing he would not be able to reach it with his hand, stuck out a foot. A burning pain shot up his leg and he collapsed to the ground. Only then did he notice that he was still wearing his bedroom slippers.

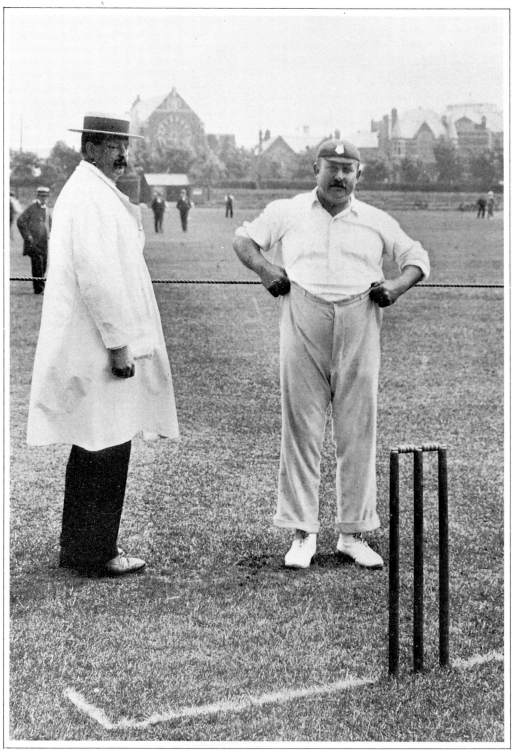

H. Baldwin of Hampshire looks as though he might have problems in his delivery stride.

When Hampshire played against Nottinghamshire in 1930 they reached a winning position late on the second day. Expecting a finish, the umpires allowed the extra half-hour but at seven o'clock, when stumps were drawn, Hampshire still required one run for victory. In the morning **the Notts side** fielded in suits and soft hats, and two players wore overcoats. The winning run was hit off the second ball of the day.

At one time an annual fixture was held between Smokers and Non Smokers. **G.J. Bonnor**, the Australian batsman, was invited to turn out for the Non Smokers, then arrived at the wicket with a large cigar in his mouth.

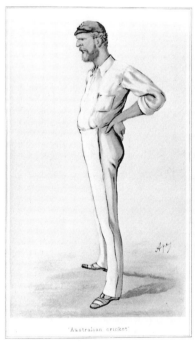

G.J. Bonnor, whom *Vanity Fair* seem to consider, by their caption, the epitome of Australian cricket.

'Australian cricket'

Syd Levey, an enthusiastic amateur who became a doyen of cricket in Port Elizabeth, South Africa, found himself going in at No 4 after the first two wickets had fallen in the opening over of the game. He opted for a policy of care and consolidation. He and his partner then played themselves in so laboriously that silly mid-on could bear the tedium no longer and lit a cigarette. Syd complained to the opposing captain who apologized and moved the man, still smoking, to silly mid-off.

Later in the match, Syd was bowling when a familiar figure came out to bat, still with a cigarette stuck in his mouth. On reaching the crease, he carefully placed the cigarette on the ground behind the stumps. Syd was not satisfied. He informed the batsman that an MCC regulation stipulated that cigarettes should be placed in front of the wicket, between the middle and off stumps – provided this did not distract the slip-fielders! The batsman did as he was told, a very confused look on his face, and was bowled next ball. Fortunately he had just enough left of his cigarette to get him back to the pavilion.

Fred Trueman showed a nice sense of balance when asked, as captain of an International Cavaliers XI, to name his batting order:

After taking 8 for 31 against India at Old Trafford in 1952, Fred Trueman tries a change of pace.

'Black, black, white, black, white, white...' said Fred, until his voice was lost beneath a gust of largely Carribean giggling.

At Bishop's Frome in Worcestershire, the eccentric feature of the 1981 season was the wicket. It was concreted over, and a green Wilton carpet laid in place of grass. **The wife of wicket-keeper David House** took on the duties of groundsperson, cleaning the carpet each week. Very little time was lost to rain.

A Hampshire village team once imported several of the county side for their annual fixture with the President's XI, and won convincingly. The following year they fielded a more normal team, but wondered if the President would retaliate. They were relieved to find an opposition consisting of several presentable club players plus a gentleman who looked very old indeed, and was readily granted a runner when he came in to bat. This ancient found it hard to hear the umpire, but soon was batting in sprightly fashion, and in fact played the decisive innings of the match.

Another year passed, the teams assembled and the village captain asked the President if he had brought along the old man who had done so well the previous year.

'Yes, there he is,' said the President, pointing to a fit and healthy young man of about thirty. He was **Ronny Aird**, of Cambridge and Hampshire (Secretary of MCC for many years and President in 1969–70), who had been expertly made up and played the part of an old man for the entire afternoon without arousing the slightest suspicion!

GOD AND CRICKET

The TCCB now recognize several forms of **Power in the Sky,** and must be broad-minded in their approach to spiritual influence both of the indirect kind, e.g. prayers for divine interference on the field of play, and the direct, e.g. actual divine interference on the field of play, whether provoked by prayer or volunteered. Respect is also needed for the mystical approach to cricket which is currently enjoying a fresh vogue, although feelings about the game have altered little since Sir James Barrie declared: 'Cricket is an idea; it is an idea of the Gods.'

A shadow of this thought must have crossed the mind of Stephen Green's West Indian correspondent. In June 1983 the curator at Lord's sent the following letter to *The Times:*
'Sir,
I do not know whether Cardinal Hume's election to membership of the MCC has any bearing on the matter but I have just had a letter from Trinidad. It was addressed to Lourdes Cricket Ground.'

The power of the medieval Church was still very much in evidence at **York Cricket Club** in the late eighteenth century. Members of the club (founded in 1784) were ordered to assemble on Heworth Moor at 4 o'clock in time for matches to start when the Minster clock struck five. Players were fined one penny for being late and this money went towards paying for a Christmas feast.

Religious discipline worked against personal glory for **Brian Rogers** of Gowerton. In 1973 he sat in the pavilion at Lord's and watched the opportunity of a lifetime pass by. Rogers, then aged 36, was the leading batsman for Gowerton CC when they reached, and narrowly lost by 12 runs, the final of the Haig National Village Cricket Championship. Had he played, his batting might have made all the difference. But, as a lay preacher at the Bethel Congregational Chapel in Gowerton, he had to insist on being left out of all Sunday matches.

In August 1969 Lancashire were hoping to acquire the services of **Vic Pollard,** the vice-captain of the New Zealand touring team. Pollard had been born in Burnley, so could be immediately available, but the county decided against signing him because, as a devout Baptist, he refused to play cricket on Sunday.

'I give that day to God,' he said to an *Observer* journalist at the Oval. 'There's no question about it. And, religious convictions aside, I don't think anybody should be asked to play cricket seven days a week.'

A thought for today?

The old-fashioned charm of the C of E was much in evidence in the 1960s at Tillingham, in rural Essex. **Old Libertians,** the Old Boys of Liberty School, Romford, played there one Rogation Sunday, a special day of supplication on behalf of the harvest.

The village team were batting in mid-innings when, along the lane, came the vicar and his congregation. Play was halted whilst the procession made its way across the outfield and on to the square. The vicar invited the players to take part in a short service. Players from both sides lined the pitch and, after an appropriate prayer, a little old lady distributed hymn books and both sides sang 'We plough the fields and scatter.' When the service was over, the procession wended its solemn way off the field and back along the lane.

Any private prayers sent up by the village team were not answered. They lost heavily.

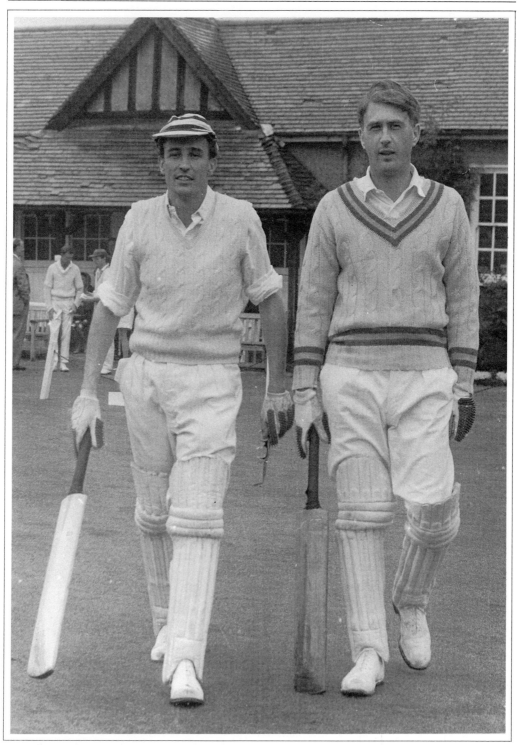

Fine weather but Divine impartiality for the 1966 Final of
the *Church Times* Cricket Cup. Rev Paul Hunt, left, and
Rev G. Farran open the innings for Liverpool.

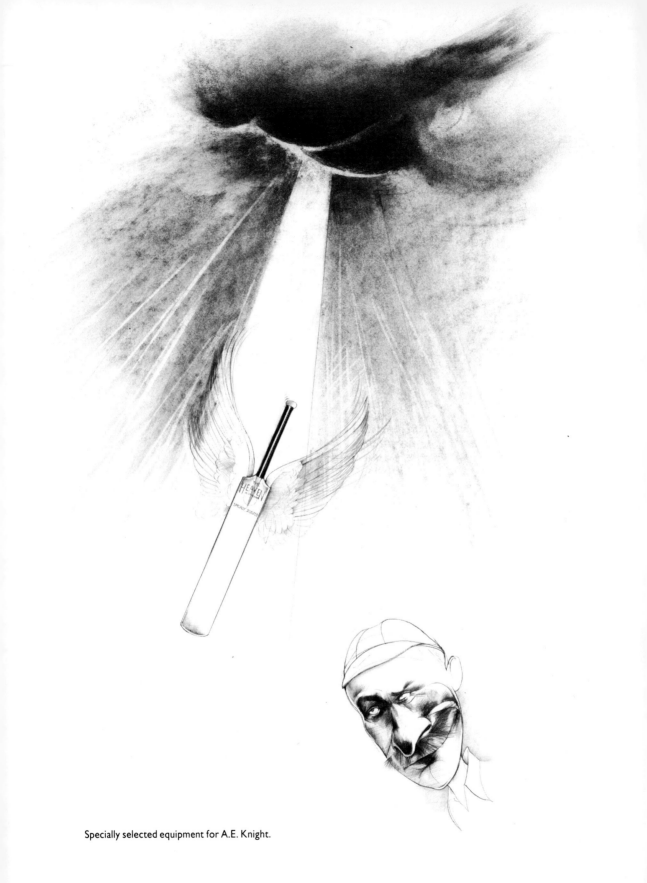

Specially selected equipment for A.E. Knight.

Pleas for divine help on the cricket field are well documented. Moreover, in an age when formal religion is said to be on the decline, it is odd to reflect that such pleas are probably uttered at most cricket matches. A particularly robust specimen was offered by **E. Wainwright,** the Yorkshire all-rounder. Before a Roses match, he knelt in the dressing-room:

'Oh, God, if You're on our side, then we'll win. If You're on their side, they'll win. But please, God, just stay out of the way for the next three days so we can thrash 'em!'

A.E. Knight, the Leicestershire and England batsman, was one of the finest players in the country prior to the First World War. He was a well-respected man, and deeply religious. Before each innings, he would offer a prayer at the crease. The Lancashire fast bowler, Walter Brearley, who hated all batsmen, complained to the MCC that Knight was attempting to gain an unfair advantage by his actions, and that there was no provision for them in the laws of the game.

Examples of direct **intervention from Above** are always interesting, but their usefulness varies in proportion to their timeliness. Something seems to have gone astray in the wristwatch department when good light stopped play in the Under-19 match between England and India at (of all places) Old Trafford in 1981. England were 28 for 0 in reply to India's 191 when they appealed against a brilliant light which, according to Umpire Gordon Gregory, 'was shining over the bowler's arm, and the batsmen couldn't see properly. They were entitled to appeal.'

Yes, but why do it in the first place? 28 for 0?

When the eminent amateur Syd Levey was on tour in Palestine in 1935, Allah pulled a nasty trick on the Jerusalem Police XI. Their opening bat was the **Inspector-General,** who batted tenaciously and reached 49. As he prepared to meet the next delivery, which was a juicy full toss, an Arab walked straight in front of the sightscreen, disturbing his concentration to such a degree that he was clean-bowled.

Instead of returning to the pavilion, the Inspector-General set off in the direction of the offender. The final act saw Allah's unfortunate instrument tearing off into the city, followed by an irate cricketer brandishing his bat!

FINANCIAL COLUMN

Cricketing wagers have been part of the game since the earliest times, and some of the stakes in those pioneering matches were fearsomely high – though in Georgian times, unlike today, betting heavily was seen as a sign of courage.

On a rather more modest scale (but not all that modest, judged by the prices of a hundred years ago) two Durham men staged a single-wicket match in 1876 in which one of them, an **innkeeper called Brown**, bet £20 that the other, an **auctioneer called Piers**, could not bowl him out in 12 hours.

The crowd that turned out to watch was highly amused when Brown appeared, and strode to the wicket holding a bat which had been made specially for the occasion and measured 10 inches across, with a blade as long as the stumps. Then Piers produced the ball he intended to use – a large heavy object more suited to the bowling green than the cricket field.

Play started at 10.50 am with Brown planting his massive bat in front of the stumps. Piers bowled the first delivery with his 27-ounce projectile, and very soon it became clear that his was the more deadly weapon. Splinters flew from Brown's bat each time contact was made, and soon the besieged innkeeper did not have enough bat to mask the whole of his wicket. Piers now aimed at an uncovered stump. Down it went, and he had won the match in less than 10 minutes.

Heroic efforts for charity had to be made in **Great Chesterford**, Essex, before even a ball could be bowled. Each time the two teams, from the local cricket club and a pub, The Plough, tried to play, down came the rain. Week after week this happened, and eventually the players decided to start at 4.30 in the morning and finish at 7 o'clock. The rain held off, 200 runs were scored and £1,000 was raised for charity. Then the players went off to work, or back to bed.

One of Britain's more famous streakers was **Michael Angelow**, a 25-year-old cook on the oil tanker *Explorer*, who jumped over both sets of stumps during the England v Australia game at Lord's in 1975. He did it for a bet, but the magistrates' fine of £20 took all his winnings.

His brother Lawrence saw him on television and said: 'It's not every day you see your brother on television, and in colour too.'

John Arlott, commentating live on radio, said: 'We have a streaker – its masculine, and not very shapely, and I should think it's seen the last of its cricket for the day.'

Michael had the last word: 'I didn't think anyone would object. The woman in the seat next to mine actually held my clothes for me.'

Benefits are intended, as the name suggests, to reward a long-serving player. Obviously when the benefit was limited to the span of just one match, rather than spread across a season as it is today, the longer the match the more the player could expect to earn from it.

Two men who defied this simple economic law, and in the process risked wrecking their own benefit, were **Albert Trott** of Middlesex and **Charlie Parker** of Gloucestershire. Against Somerset in 1907 Trott dismissed four Somerset batsmen in five

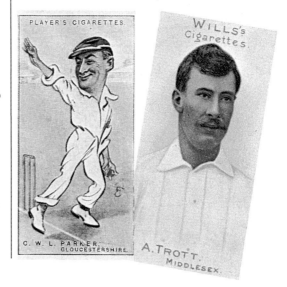

balls, then followed up with a second hat-trick in the same innings. Parker almost went one better. Playing against Yorkshire at Bristol in 1922, he considerably shortened his own benefit match by taking 9 for 36, and hitting the stumps with five consecutive balls. The second of these, however, was a no-ball.

Establishing the correct rate for the job of playing cricket has troubled players and committees alike since the beginnings of the organized game. When **Bobby Abel** made 357 not out for Surrey against Somerset at the Oval in 1899, Surrey were paying their professionals £1 for every fifty runs. The county committee then held an urgent discussion and decided that the bonus should carry a top limit of £5. Abel was so incensed that he told the committee he would never bother going beyond 250 again. He never did.

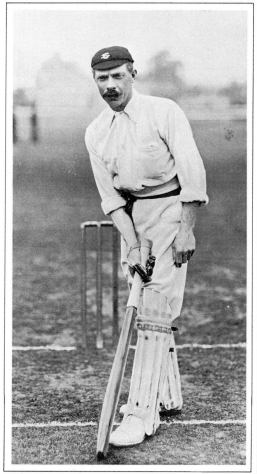

Bobby Abel – no incentive, no runs.

George Gunn, the great Nottinghamshire opening batsman, was almost a law unto himself. He was also something of a hypochondriac, and the poor state of his health was regularly offered as his excuse for getting out cheaply. He was particularly concerned with the behaviour of his digestive system.

He saw the lunch-break as a pillar supporting much of the surrounding day; as such it was surely immovable from its traditional starting-time of 1.30 pm. One day Notts were playing Glamorgan at Cardiff. Gunn's score was in the eighties when 1.30 arrived. At the end of what he took to be the final over before lunch, Gunn turned for the pavilion. The umpire called him back and told him that it had been specially agreed to take lunch that day at 2 o'clock.

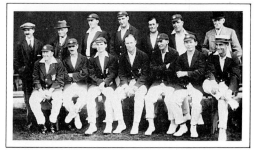

George Gunn seated on the left of his captain, A.W. Carr, in the Notts side of 1922.

Gunn was most indignant. Facing the next ball, a straight delivery, he raised his bat high and allowed the ball to hit the wicket. Now A.W. Carr, his captain, was equally furious, and when Gunn reached the pavilion demanded what he thought he was up to.

'Well, Mr Carr,' replied Gunn, 'me digestion expects its vittles at half-past one, and I don't see why today should be any different.'

Gunn was also adept at striking a bargain if he had to work harder than usual. Some of the Notts team were involved in a motoring accident on the way to play Yorkshire at Headingly, and all the bowlers were injured. Luckily Carr won the toss and could choose to bat first, to give his bowlers time to recover. He told Gunn at all costs to stay at the wicket until tea-time but Gunn, no longer a youngster, protested that this was asking too much.

Carr would not reduce his demand and was still at the crease but so tired that he Gunn agreed, but only if he was paid £1 an hour above his usual wages. At 3.30 pm he

delivered an ultimatum. He wanted time and a
half for holding out until 5.30 pm. Once more
Carr agreed, and Gunn continued majestically
to hold the fort, scoring steadily at the rate of
30 runs an hour until the day was saved
beyond doubt.

MASTERS OF CEREMONY

E.M. Grace, the Gloucestershire secretary for many years during the nineteenth century, was not a man to bother with convention. The minutes of a club meeting in 1873 read: 'Committee meeting held at the White Lion Hotel, Bristol, on Thursday 25 at 3 o'clock. Present: E.M. Grace and that's all.'

At least he did not have to contend with the farmer who owned the land on which East Sussex club **Upper Dicker** have played for more than two hundred years. Ern Smith, a local veteran, explained:

'The outfield used to be a bit slow. The farmer wouldn't let us cut the grass until the end of July.'

Matches during June and July must have been interesting! That farmer is in charge no longer, by the way, and the field is now very trim.

Ern himself had further direct experience of how difficult farmers can be. His employer, who was also his father, sacked him for playing too much cricket!

The problem at **Darfield,** near Barnsley, was to protect the windows of houses in Cover Drive (!) from the local six-hitters. Barnsley Council approved the fitting of special windows at a cost of more than £2000. A Council spokesman said:

'The windows will stop cricket balls and a bullet from a small rifle.'

Cricket's own administrators rarely get themselves in such a twist as the **South African Board** in 1938. It had earlier been agreed by both sides that the final Test of the series should be played to a finish. After ten days, England had reached 654 for 5, chasing a remarkable target of 696. At this point the South African Board declared that 'in consultation with the captains, the match shall be abandoned at 5.45 because the Board recognizes that the players in the MCC team would not have enough time left to travel from Durban to Cape Town to catch the boat home.'

Said a disappointed Wally Hammond: 'These games are *not* in the best interests of cricket.'

Selectors can be accused of various inadequacies, especially when the team fails to win. One of the most eccentric selectorial meetings of all time occurred in 1956. England were trailing Australia by 1–0 after two Tests, and had problems with their batting. The selectors had thought of everyone. Then one of the selectors, **Cyril Washbrook,** was asked to leave the room. On his return, he was informed that he himself had been selected!

Days later he went to the wicket with England on 17 for 3, but rescued the innings with a fine 98; Peter May scored 101, and

Peter May in uncharacteristically awkward pose, but Cyril Washbrook, right, still looks untroubled in 1958, two years after his famous recall to Test cricket.

England went on to win the match, and eventually the series by 2–1, though not before the unconventional, if not eccentric, selection committee had sprung further surprises by bringing back David Sheppard and Denis Compton. Sheppard celebrated with 113, Compton with 90.

Other players have had cause to wonder how the mind of a selector works. **Andy Ganteaume** scored 112 for the West Indies on his Test début against England in 1948 at Port of Spain; he was never again selected for his country. Nor was **Rodney Redmond** of New Zealand, who on his Test début in 1973 scored 107 and 56 against Pakistan at

Auckland. **C.S. Marriott** was another who fell dramatically from favour. Against the West Indies in 1933, Marriott's leg-spinners earned him 5 for 37 and 6 for 59 in a match that England won by an innings and 117 runs; he was never again selected for his country.

The luckless C.S. Marriott.

The Chairman of the Selectors is supposed to be the man in charge but **Alec Bedser** was no doubt covered in confusion when he phoned Mike Brearley to tell him that he had been recalled to captain England, after the resignation of Ian Botham, in 1981.

Brearley's view of the call; 'I picked the phone up several times at my flat. Each time I heard pips: in the end the operator asked me if I would pay for the call, and that's how I found out.'

As an administrator, **Martin,** (whose surname shall remain anonymous), the former captain of the Rejects CC, was in a class of his own. Like all leaders of the Rejects, he was as old as Viv Richards's career average, distinctly unathletic but obsessed with cricket.

A university lecturer by profession, he inherited a middling-to-large sum of money and used it to purchase a delapidated country mansion, luring thither his university's groundsman with instructions to turn a

waterlogged meadow into a cricket pitch. The groundsman achieved the near-impossible, and next season matches were being played on 'Martin's Green' – although, after rain, the bounce tended to be unpredictable.

Not surprisingly, shortly after he offered them the free use of his pitch, Martin became captain of the Rejects. Soon, teams were changing in the library, among mouldering sermons and rotting manuals on horse-breeding. Clothes were hung over busts of Shakespeare and Dickens. At the end of the match, the opposition trooped off to the banqueting hall, expecting at least a 'knife-and-fork do' with, possibly, mulled ale or mead, followed by an evening's entertainment from minstrels and the court jester. What they usually got, if they were lucky, was a digestive biscuit and a jam jar half-full of a nauseous mixture of cocoa and orange-juice.

The wicket at Martin's Green was rolled by patients from a nearby institution where Martin sometimes lectured. These patients did a fine job, and were rewarded by being allowed to bowl in the nets to new Rejects recruits. This was part of Martin's initiation test for all prospective members. No helmets, pads, gloves or boxes were allowed. 'They just slow down your reflexes,' explained Martin, who stood in judgment at a respectful distance as the bowlers advanced *en masse* and began hurling beamers, bouncers and short-pitched deliveries, simultaneously, and mostly with suspect arm-actions, from fifteen yards.

In the event of England losing the first two Test Matches, we believe it is the intention of the Selection Committee to invite the above players to start practising.

Most recruits were soon crouching in a corner of the net begging for mercy. The few who survived were allowed by Martin to become members, with the prospect of being picked for every match. As may be imagined, the membership of Rejects CC was somewhat limited; several unsuccessful recruits became, through their failure to qualify, inmates of this same institution, and later were allowed to be net bowlers themselves, which perhaps explains their ferocity.

As captain, Martin was responsible for sorting out the arrangements for the Annual Dinner. These duties included collecting the trophies from previous winners, having them polished, engraved and made ready for presentation. One year, in the middle of the turkey, Martin hurriedly left the table; moments later his car headlights were seen shooting away down the drive.

He was gone a long time and the Secretary was filling in desperately when Martin returned laden with trophies. These he piled on the top table and proceeded to present. It was soon realized, except by Martin, that something was amiss. The leading batsman's trophy was topped by a statuette of a fisherman complete with rod and line; the Fielder of the Year took away a fine trophy surmounted by a couple doing the foxtrot; the wicket-keeper became the proud possessor of a giant comb on a plinth inscribed 'Hairdresser Grade One'.

Martin had driven round the houses of the previous winners and blindly raided every sideboard he came upon. There had been no time to check the inscriptions, so he had snatched up all the available trophies and hurtled back to the dinner.

1921 was not a good year for England's selectors. When defeat looked imminent in the 2nd Test against Warwick Armstrong's powerful Australians, the cartoonists were already seeing problems ahead and suggesting their own solution.

NOT QUITE HIMSELF

Another four byes? Bob Taylor seems intent on breaking the Kent record.

Eccentric deeds, both on the field and off it, may well be the by-product of some injury, suspected or otherwise; they may also be induced by the too-rapid dispersal through the system of alcohol.

Tony Catt, who had to wait in the wings during most of his career for Kent because of the brilliance of Godfrey Evans, was mainly responsible for the record number of extras conceded in first class cricket – 75 (48 byes, 23 leg-byes, 2 wides) v Northants in 1955. When he came off the field, the unlucky Catt was found to be suffering from severe sunstroke.

Charlie Harris, the famous Notts batsman, found himself in hospital one day with a dislocated shoulder, after an accident in the field. He was protesting loudly when the Sister said:

'Mr Harris, you're making a dreadful fuss of having your shoulder put back. There's a woman downstairs who has just had twins, and she's making far less noise than you.'

'That may be,' said Harris, 'but you try putting the twins back, and see what she says.'

From an 1841 edition of the *Wiltshire and Gloucestershire Standard* comes this report:

'The Rev. Pickering, one of the masters at Eton, met with a serious accident last week. He and his friends were using a bowling machine called a "catapult", worked by powerful steel springs and able to project the ball unerringly towards the batter. By some mismanagement, the springs went off and the lever, striking Mr Pickering with uncommon force, laid him prostrate. His right cheek was laid open to the upper lip to the extent of some inches. His life is now out of danger.'

C.C. Case, when playing for Somerset against Nottinghamshire at Taunton in 1930, was dismissed 'hit wicket' by Bill Voce, after collapsing on to his stumps. So disoriented was he that he marched off to the pavilion carrying a stump instead of his bat.

Phil King, a Yorkshireman who had played with Worcestershire before the Second World War, played for two seasons with Lancashire after the war. King, a burly man who also played Rugby League, was batting against Kent at Old Trafford, when a vicious delivery from one of the Kent fast bowlers rose off a length and hit him full on the 'box'. King collapsed in agony on the pitch and, after some moments of profanity, unbuttoned his flies to inspect any possible damage. Alarmed, his batting partner came down the wicket and urgently warned him:

'Phil! You can't do that. There are ten thousand here.'

'Blow the ten thousand,' King groaned, 'I've only got one of these.'

A **well-known eccentric** on the Kent and Sussex club circuit was renowned for his cavalier approach to the game. A friend recalls:

'I first met him at Rye where the ground was under the sea 100 years ago and it is necessary to check on the tide before tossing up. It rained all morning and we couldn't start until after lunch. My own club were on tour in Kent and Sussex and we were very impressed with Tony's generosity in buying drinks for everyone and consuming an inordinate amount of gin for his own lunch. We assumed he must be a gentleman farmer and were somewhat intrigued to hear that he was a schoolmaster. However, his school was for the very backward sons of the very rich!

'At 3 pm I opened the batting and Tony opened the bowling. His first three deliveries raised three tiny divots in a tight triangle on the good-length spot. I drew his attention to this accuracy and he replied:

'"Dear boy, I can't see you, I can't see the stumps. I'm aiming for that big white board behind you!"'

Cricketing schoolmasters frequently *are* eccentric. Some go to extremes in enforcing the correct *approach* to the game which they often consider more important than actually teaching the art of playing it. A prep-school headmaster in Surrey beat the school captain not because he had made a duck but because, on his way back to the pavilion, he had

practised the correct playing of the stroke which had got him out. This, apparently was not the cricket etiquette which the headmaster adhered to.

Another headmaster, Dr Heath of Eton, is said to have flogged every member of the school eleven defeated by Westminster.

The master in charge of cricket at a prep-school in Eastbourne had instilled into his pupils the importance of taking quick singles. The non-strikers were instructed to back up a good way down the pitch, in theory starting their movement after the ball had left the bowler's hand. The instructions were not strictly followed, however, and in a match against a school called Harewood in 1956, no fewer than seven members of the team were run out as they backed up.

The cricket masters of two other prep schools, Feltonfleet and Belmont (both in Surrey), were better at teaching cricket than they were at organizing fixtures. One warm Saturday afternoon both were waiting impatiently with their bright-eyed teams ready for the start of a match against one of their old rivals. By two-fifteen the opposition had failed to arrive, though the match was due to begin at two o'clock. Suddenly the Belmont master had a twinge of conscience. He must have got his fixtures muddled. Perhaps the game was *away*, not at home. Quickly he hustled the boys into the rather delapidated school bus and made haste towards Cobham. Meanwhile, exactly the same feelings of embarrassment and remorse were going through the mind of his opposite number at Feltonfleet. *Of course*, that was the answer. It must be an away match. He phoned Belmont but got no reply, since everyone else was out on the school grounds watching other matches. Wasting no further time, he bustled his team into the school's slightly more modern mini-bus. Five miles outside Cobham, down a twisting country lane, his vehicle was in collision with another, larger, school bus, travelling at great speed in the other direction . . . a meeting of two cricket teams which had certainly not been intended.

The hero of the school cricket team used to be one of the principal characters in Boys Own and other similar boys papers. One real school hero at Marlborough College in 1926 got a slightly inflated opinion of his own abilities (which were indeed considerable because he became a first-class cricketer of note) and the cricket master, T.C.G. 'Sandy' Sandford, who

Allan Lamb and Derek Randall, right, feel the pressures of
international cricket.

believed in teaching not just the principles of technique but also of modesty and correct behaviour, set out to reduce the size of the boy's swollen head. Once a week it was customary for the star of the team to stay on after the first eleven had practised for a net of his own against Sandy, an accomplished spin bowler, and the school professional, Dave Jennings, also a spin bowler of great accuracy. Large crowds of admiring boys would watch these weekly sessions, with the infant prodigy, S.A. Block, usually mastering his more experienced opponents with great ease.

One sunny afternoon, however, on the usual perfect-looking net wicket, he was suddenly made to look like a novice and a fool. Pushing forward confidently to the first well-flighted leg-break he was amazed to see the ball leap off the placid pitch and remove the top of his off stump. The next ball fizzed back and struck him in the box. Soon he was reduced to impotence (cricketing impotence, that is) and he left the net half an hour later, having been out time and again, crestfallen.

During the lunch hour Sandy had carefully cut a two foot square out of the turf, removed the firm sub-soil and filled the area with loose earth. Then he had replaced the turf so that the surface appeared perfectly normal. Both Sandy and Dave were accurate enough to hit the loose earth often enough to cut the hero down to size. Eccentric, but successful; for in spite of major successes at cricket, rugby and hockey, 'Spenner' Block never again manifested conceit.

The great Nottinghamshire fast-bowler **John Jackson** stood six feet tall and weighed over fifteen stone. He would fix the incoming batsman with a stare and each time he took a wicket would celebrate by blowing his nose loudly. This habit inspired the nickname 'Foghorn' Jackson, which stayed with him until his death in 1901.

His nose was noticeably one-sided after an accident in the nets at Cambridge. On that occasion brandy was brought from the pavilion to rub into the injured nose, but Jackson knew better:

'I drank the brandy,' he said, 'and went to the pavilion for hot water!'

ECCENTRIC ENDINGS

The chances of an eccentric ending to a match are always helped by a tight finish. The atmosphere tautens, and collectors of eccentric moments peer round the field wondering if someone, or something, will snap.

A recent match between **two Cheshire County League sides** had an amazing conclusion. When the teams, from opposite ends of the league, met, the well-placed team made 220. The opposition, while thinking the match was well out of their reach, gave it a go, and were 150 for 4 before a collapse saw three wickets fall cheaply. However, the eighth-wicket partnership took them to within sight of a famous victory. When the ninth wicket fell off the second ball of the last over, the underdogs needed just two runs to win. In came the last man.

His own team had little confidence in him. A week earlier he had managed, unintentionally, to get locked in behind the bar of his own clubhouse. The third and fourth balls brought no score. The fifth ball struck our hero on the pad, but was well off target and the fielding side did not even bother to appeal. To their amazement, the batsman straightened up and headed towards the pavilion.

'What are you doing?' an opponent

asked him.

'I know when I'm out,' he answered.

'But you've not been given out!'

'I think I was out, and that's all that matters.'

The umpires had no choice but to let him go. The scorebook reads 'retired out' and the match was lost by one run.

No amount of persuasion could convince the No 11 afterwards that he had been over-hasty. The victors gladly took the points and went on to win the league.

By contrast, calmness under fire was the hallmark of a conversation between the **captain of Wimbledon CC** and a schoolboy who was playing for the 3rd XI during the summer holidays.

'How did you get on?' asked the captain.

'Oh, we won. It was a great game. We bowled them out for 21 and scored 22 for 9.'

'Who got the runs then?'

Immense controversy surrounded a recent county league game. With the visitors' last pair at the wicket, and with four runs needed to win, the home team's bowler hit the stumps, and the ball went down to third man. In the meantime the umpire had called 'no ball'. A spectator, believing the game to be over, walked onto the field, picked up the ball and threw it neatly back to the wicket-keeper.

The umpire awarded the batting side four runs, and so they won the match by one wicket.

By their all-or-nothing nature, single-wicket matches are well geared to the eccentric ending. In the early years of this century a contest was arranged between **C.H.G. Bland** of Sussex and **W.M. Bradley,** the Kent and England fast bowler. K.S. Ranjitsinhji agreed to umpire. Bland batted all day, and as night fell Bradley had still not taken his wicket, so the match was abandoned.

Dogs are particularly good at this form of cricket. In a single-wicket match played on Harefield Common near Rickmansworth in 1927, two Gentlemen of Middlesex challenged a local farmer, **Mr Francis Trumper,** to find a partner for a challenge match between pairs. Mr Trumper chose his dog. In the first innings the two Gentlemen scored three runs, and Mr Trumper scored five. In the second innings the two Gentlemen again scored three runs, leaving Mr Trumper to score two runs for victory, which he did.

At the start of the match the betting had

W.M. Bradley as he may well have looked after bowling all day at C.H.G. Bland, right.

been 5 to 1 against Trumper and his partner. However, what swung the match was the brilliant fielding of the dog, who ran up with his master as he bowled and followed the ball so quickly down the pitch that his jaws closed on it almost immediately after it was struck. Try as they might, the two Gentlemen had the greatest difficulty in getting the ball away, and could only amass six runs

It is not always enough merely to add a dog's name to the team-sheet. In a challenge match on Streatham Common a one-armed man put himself up against **Silas Quarterman,** who kept an inn on the edge of the common. As a means of balancing the contest, it was agreed that the one-armed man should have the assistance of his 10-year-old son, while Quarterman was allowed

to field his well-trained dog.

It was a good match, narrowly won by the one-armed challenger. The turning-point came when the dog made an excellent stop but, instead of returning the ball to its master, dashed off in the opposite direction and did not stop until it had reached the inn, nearly two miles away!

The 'Irish' method of settling rained-off matches by having all 22 players bowl at unprotected stumps is now widely used, and is allowed for in the rules of the National Village Championship organized by *The Cricketer.* In 1979, Scottish clubs **Rossie Priory** and **Fochabers** also settled their match in this way. After all 11 men on each

Another enthusiastic fielder. This shaggy substitute offered
his services during the 2nd Test at Christchurch in 1984
but New Zealand needed little outside help in their
historic win over England.

team had bowled, the score was 2–2, and eventually, after 66 balls, Priory won 9–6.

On another occasion in Kent, the score was 0–0 after 21 balls, and the issue was decided by one of the wicket-keepers. He ran up, dropped the ball almost at his feet and saw it trundle down the wicket . . . and just dislodge the leg bail.

An eccentric ending to a tour was the reward of the triumphant England team which retained the Ashes in 1979. They flew into Heathrow Airport to be met by a demonstrating mob of punks. Their leader, **Captain Sensible of The Damned,** informed them:

'We are the only true supporters of English cricket, and we are appalled at the treatment of Geoffrey Boycott by Mike Brearley. He is the hero of punks across the country, and he can have a free ticket to any of my concerts, any time. In fact, all the team can, except Brearley.'

Another of the punks, Christy Kistener, an 18-year-old from Nuremburg, West Germany, said: 'We came here to catch a glimpse of Geoff. Back in Germany he is the only cricketer that the Germans know about.'

Neither Boycott nor Brearley was on the flight.

Eccentric strike action in Poona brought a sad ending to the innings of **B.B. Nimbalkar** of Maharashtra in the 1948–49 season. With 443 runs to his credit, he was within 9 of Don Bradman's then world record innings of 452 not out. Lunch was taken and Nimbalkar was full of confidence that the record would soon be his. He was justifiably staggered when Kathiawar, the fielding side, refused to take the field after lunch. They said they had had enough, conceded the match and went home.

Many an innings has ended suddenly through catastrophic running between the wickets, and the departing batsman may be forgiven if at times he fails to suppress his disappointment. Two well-known characters in the St Lawrence, Canterbury side in the late 1940s were **Gordon Heyer** and **Ralph Kemp.** They were batting quietly together against Dover when Kemp drove a ball into the covers, called and started to run. To his dismay, Heyer did not move and Kemp, skidding to turn round, failed to make his

ground and was run out. He departed with a dejected look on his face and had almost reached the pavilion when he stopped, returned to where Heyer was standing and said:

'Gordon, I don't mind being run out but I hate to be bloody well ignored.'

He turned again for the pavilion, leaving the fielding side convulsed.

At a dinner held in 1967 to commemorate **Frank Woolley's** 80th birthday, **J.G.W. Davies** recounted a similar story:

'I was invited to play for Kent in the Canterbury Week, having had a successful Varsity season. This was the ultimate. On the first morning, when it came to be my turn to bat, Frank was in. This made me so proud. In no time I played a ball into the covers, called "One" and ran. When I looked up, Frank was chatting to the umpire. I turned back, dived full-length, getting filthy, but was run out. With head bowed I returned to the pavilion, near to tears. I sat in the dressing-room with my pads on until lunchtime. All the other players went to lunch and Frank Woolley came in, still not out. Surely he will speak, I thought, but no. He took off his pads, washed his hands, combed his hair, put on his blazer and went out without saying a word. I was still sitting there when the door opened and Frank put his head in. "You were in a blooming hurry this morning," he said, and departed again.'

F.E. WOOLLEY

Jock Livingston, the New South Wales and Northants batsman, claimed that he was so careful in accepting singles that he was only run out once. On that occasion the ball hit a submerged metal water point, and flew straight into a fielder's hands.

A small misunderstanding.

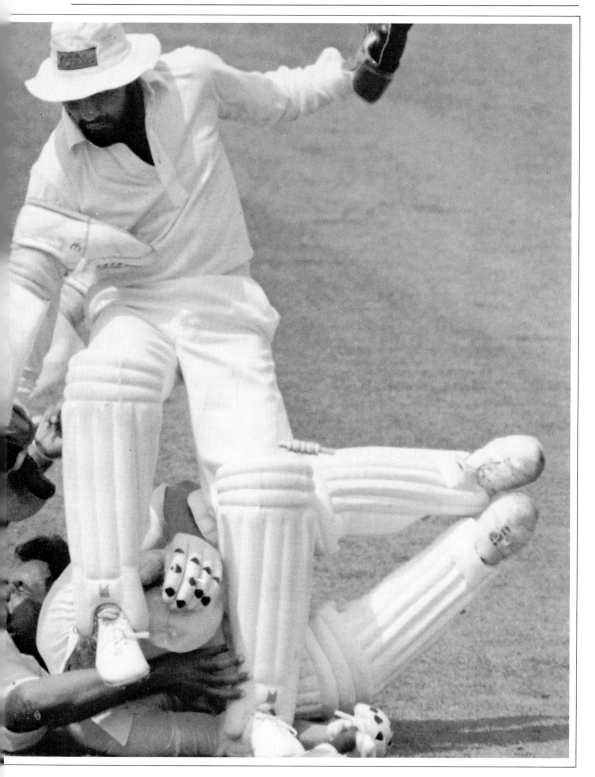

"DUCKS."

Some unfortunate endings as seen by Hiscocks in *The Cricketer*, 1921.

An extraordinary run-out occurred in 1922 when **'Crusoe' Robertson Glasgow** and **Tom Raikes** were playing for Oxford against Surrey. Having met in mid-pitch, they ran side by side for the next four runs 'as though attached to a harness'. The wickets were already flattened, then someone had the sense to grab a stump and uproot it with the ball in the same hand. The umpires, totally confused, could not decide who was out. The problem was resolved by tossing a coin, and Raikes was declared out.

Possibly the world's worst running episode concerned **Ali Bacher,** the former South African captain, in a club match for Balfour Park. He was batting with Archer Wilson, who hit the ball into the covers, and both batsmen started on a quick single.

Halfway down the track, Wilson called 'No' and turned back. Both batsmen were heading for the striker's wicket, and both made their ground. The ball was sent immediately to the bowler's end, and the bowler, doubtless surprised by finding both batsmen heading towards him, broke the wicket without the ball in his hand.

The batsmen then split up, Wilson heading for the 'keeper's end and Bacher staying put. But then communications between 'keeper and bowler broke down, and Bacher and Wilson were tempted out of their respective creases. Further cries of 'Yes,' 'No,' 'Wait,' 'Sorry', ensued, and by the time order had been restored, the batsmen were still not out but both had run more than 100 yards, both sets of stumps were flat on the ground, and not a run had been scored!

HORACE

In the old days, before the club moved to its present ground, the members played on a pitch at the bottom end of the village green. The square was in the sole charge of **Horace.**

Although at least middle-aged, he was extremely active, with an independent mind. He alone decided when the outfield was short enough; he decreed when the pitch was flat and true; he knew when it was time for a rest and a drink.

On away match-days he was always the first to be ready, waiting for the others to help load up the kit and the crates of ale.

They never hurried along the country lanes, knowing from years of experience the time needed to reach the various village grounds.

On the return trip, Horace picked out the pubs to stop at – the crated ale having been finished on the outward journey.

He imbibed as much as any of them, and often felt the narrow lanes sway and the hedgerows brush his face. But in those days the lanes were traffic-free, and there were no breath-tests.

Back in the village, Horace was often the only one who could remember where they all lived, and he dutifully saw them all home and got their kit unloaded.

He enjoyed away matches, never missed one all season – even though, so far, they'd never asked him to play.

Tomorrow was a rest-day, time to clear the head, then there was next week's wicket to prepare.

Horace looked forward to cutting the outfield, and then moving on to his favourite activity, working with the roller, for which he put on special canvas shoes so that his hooves would not harm the wicket.

Karachi's answer to Horace receives a guiding hand from Bob Taylor.

Acknowledgments
The publishers would like to acknowledge with
thanks the help given by the following who supplied
the stories around which this book has been
developed:

J.F. Burrell, Aubrey Bush, James D. Coldham,
Colin Cracknell, Anandji Dossa, A. Evans,
Peter Hargreaves/Tom Provis, G.A. Hodcroft, John
Hollinshead, Roger Mann, George Mell,
W.T. Moore, Tony Moss, J.F. Reece,
Colin Sandford, J.G. Senior, Charles Steggell,
Reg Woodward.

The publishers also thank the following sources for
their help in providing illustrations:

Central Press, Keystone Press Agency,
Marylebone Cricket Club,
Adrian Murrell/Allsport Photographic.